Dominican Republic

by Lee Karen Stow

Award-winning travel journalist and photographer Lee Karen Stow travels widely and regularly for a number of national newspapers, magazines and adventure travel books. Lee lives in East Yorkshire, England, she loves the outdoors and is a keen scuba diver and horse rider.

Above: *a half-moon of sand beckons on the uncrowded southwest coast*

AA Publishing

Above: *musical quartet at Altos de Chavón*

Written by Lee Karen Stow

First published 2001
Reprinted Aug 2002

Reprinted 2004. Information updated and verified.

Published by AA Publishing, a trading name of Automobile Association Developments Limited, whose registered office is Millstream, Maidenhead Road, Windsor, Berkshire SL4 5GD.
Registered number 1878835.

A CIP catalogue record for this book is available from the British Library.

The contents of this publication are believed correct at the time of printing. Nevertheless, AA Publishing accept no responsibility for errors, omissions or changes in the details given, or for the consequences of readers' reliance on this information. This does not affect your statutory rights. Assessments of attractions, hotels and restaurants are based upon the author's own experience and contain subjective opinions that may not reflect the publisher's opinion or a reader's experience. We have tried to ensure accuracy, but things do change, so please let us know if you have any comments or corrections.

Find out more about AA Publishing and the wide range of travel publications and services the AA provides by visiting our website at www.theAA.com

A01641

Colour separation: Chroma Graphics (Overseas) Pte Ltd, Singapore
Printed and bound in Italy by Printer Trento S.r.l.

Contents

About this Book 4

Viewing the Dominican Republic 5–10
- Lee Karen Stow's Dominican Republic 6
- The 10 Essentials 7
- The Shaping of the Dominican Republic 8
- Peace and Quiet 9
- The Dominican Republic's Famous 10

Top Ten 11–22
- Altos de Chavón 12
- Bahía de Samaná 13
- Cordillera Central 14–15
- Isla Saona 16
- Lago Enriquillo 17
- Monumento a los Héroes, Santiago 18
- Parque Nacional La Isabela 19
- Playa Boca Chica 20
- Puerto Plata 21
- Zona Colonial, Santo Domingo 22

What to See 23–72
- Santo Domingo 26–37
- In the Know 38–39
- Around the Country 40–72
- Food and Drink 48–49

Where To... 73–86
- Eat and Drink 74–76
- Stay 77–79
- Shop 80–81
- Be Entertained 82–86

Practical Matters 87–92

Index 93–4

Acknowledgements 94

About this Book

KEY TO SYMBOLS

- map reference to the maps found in the What to See section
- address or location
- telephone number
- opening times
- restaurant or café on premises or near by
- nearest bus/tram route
- ferry crossings and boat excursions
- tourist information
- facilities for visitors with disabilities
- admission charge
- other places of interest near by
- other practical information
- ➤ indicates the page where you will find a fuller description
- travel by air

This book is divided into five sections to cover the most important aspects of your visit to the Dominican Republic.

Viewing the Dominican Republic pages 5–11
An introduction to Dominican Republic by the author.

The 10 Essentials
The Shaping of the Dominican Republic
Peace and Quiet
The Dominican Republic's Famous

Top Ten pages 11–22
The author's choice of the Top Ten places to see in the Dominican Republic, each with practical information.

What to See pages 23–72
The five main areas of the Dominican Republic, each with its own brief introduction and an alphabetical listing of the main attractions.

Practical information
Snippets of 'Did you know…' information
7 suggested walks, drives and excursions
2 features

Where To… pages 73–86
Detailed listings of the best places to eat, stay, shop, take the children and be entertained.

Practical Matters pages 87–92
A highly visual section containing essential travel information.

Maps
All map references are to the individual maps found in the What to See section of this guide.

For example, Parque Nacional Monte Cristi has the reference 24A4 – indicating the page on which the map is located and the grid square in which the national park is to be found. A list of the maps that have been used in this travel guide can be found in the index.

Prices
Where appropriate, an indication of the cost of an establishment is given by **£** signs:

£££ denotes higher prices, **££** denotes average prices, while **£** denotes lower charges.

Star Ratings
Most of the places described in this book have been given a separate rating:

✪✪✪	Do not miss
✪✪	Highly recommended
✪	Worth seeing

Viewing the Dominican Republic

Lee Karen Stow's Dominican Republic	6
The 10 Essentials	7
The Shaping of the Dominican Republic	8
Peace and Quiet	9
The Dominican Republic's Famous	10

Above: *windsurfing boards line up on the white sands of Punta Cana in the south*
Right: *a popular means of transport for the locals*

Lee Karen Stow's Dominican Republic

Geographical Facts
The Dominican Republic (Republica Dominica) makes up two thirds of the island of Hispaniola, the second largest island of the Greater Antilles. It shares the island with Haiti to the west and is bordered to the north by the Atlantic Ocean, and the Caribbean Sea in the south. Estimates suggest a population of almost 8 million.

Below: *adventure in the mountains, rafting on the Río Yaque del Norte*
Inset: *tall palms at Punta Cana*

Palm-lined beaches, engulfed by aquamarine waters and backed by fertile tropical vegetation, first tempted the gold-seeking explorer, Christopher Columbus, to set foot upon the Dominican Republic's shores.

These days holidaymakers arrive to pulsating *merengue* music before being whisked off to all-inclusive resorts and hotels as big as towns along developed coastlines. New resorts have been inching their way onto virgin sands since organised tourism began here in the 1950s. In recent years transport has improved and a drive to establish eco-tourism and adventure tourism has resulted in off-the-beaten-track activities and a chance to observe the country's flora and fauna.

In the baked desert of the southwest wildlife safaris take you across lakes as smooth as glass, to spot crocodiles and flamingos. National parks brim with birds, reptiles, butterflies and flora. You can learn Spanish, surf like a champion or photograph waterfalls. In the capital, Santo Domingo, trails follow the footsteps of the Spanish who established the first city in the New World, a base from which to conquer the Americas and now a World Heritage Site. To escape the heat, take a jeep safari into the interior of flamboyant trees and pine forests, where strawberries and coffee grow. Here, among the Caribbean's tallest mountains, rises Pico Duarte at 3,175m, the anchor of the Dominican Alps. Variety is being pushed as the Dominican Republic's spice of life. If it's all too much for you though, there's always the beach.

THE 10 ESSENTIALS

If you only have a short time to visit the Dominican Republic, or would like to get a complete picture of the country, here are the essentials:

- **Go whale-watching** in the Bahía de Samaná (Samana Bay) (▶ 13) and watch humpback whales breach spectacularly from the ocean (▶ 54).
- **Walk the cobbled streets of the historic Zona Colonial** in the capital, Santo Domingo, where the Spanish conquistadors established their mighty seat in the New World (▶ 22, 32).
- **Laze on the white sands** of the Atlantic coast, doing nothing more than ordering rum punches.
- **Take a speedboat** through crystal waters to Isla Saona (Saona Island) (▶ 16, 60) in the Parque Nacional de la Este (National Park of the East) (▶ 59) to swim, then eat grilled lobster beneath the shade of a palm.
- **Learn to windsurf** with the experts on world-famous Cabarete beach (▶ 41, 85).
- **Breathe in the invigorating alpine air** in the foothills of Pico Duarte, the Caribbean's tallest mountain (▶ 70).
- **Have your hair braided** and adorned with beads. Yes, men too. And don't forget to barter.
- **Watch cigars being made** at tobacco museums in the Cibao Valley, then buy one to smoke after dinner.
- **Spot American crocodiles and pink flamingos** at Lago Enriquillo (Lake Enriquillo) and don't forget a camera (▶ 17).
- **Learn to dance *merengue* like a Dominican,** then get totally carried away on the dance floor.

Above: *sail boards stand ready at the windsurfing capital of Cabarete*
Below: *Dominican children are often happy to be photographed*

The Shaping of the Dominican Republic

Navigator and explorer, Christopher Columbus

AD *c*800
Arawak Indians (later Tainos) arrive in canoes from the South American mainland.

1492
In December the *Santa María* runs aground on the north of the island. Captain Christopher Columbus names the island La Isla Española (Hispaniola) in honour of Queen Isabella of Spain. A quest for gold is begun. It takes just 30 years for the Tainos to be wiped out by disease, slavery and suicide.

1498
Columbus's brother, Bartolomé, establishes Nueva Isabella near modern-day Santo Domingo.

1697 and 1795
Spain cedes (western then eastern) Hispaniola to France.

1809
Spanish rule is restored.

1821–2
Haitian troops seize control of the country.

1844
On February 27 Juan Pablo Duarte leads a revolt against the Haitians. Independence is won.

1916–1924
US Marines occupy the country.

1930
Rafael Leonidas Trujillo, chief of the former Dominican National Police, comes to power. A ruthless dictator, he erects extravagant monuments to himself and kills or tortures his critics.

1961
Trujillo is assassinated.

1962
Juan Bosch becomes the first democratically elected president.

1963
Bosch is overthrown. Years of controversial elections follow.

1992
President Joaquin Balaguer orders the Faro a Colón monument to be built to mark the the 500th anniversary of Colombus's landing.

2000
Hipólito Mejía of the Dominican Revolutionary Party elected president.

2002
Haitian President Jean-Bertrand Aristide makes an historic visit to discuss co-operation between the neighbours.

Statue of Juan Pablo Duarte in Santo Domingo

Peace & Quiet

The reputation of the Dominican Republic's natural beauty is growing, despite rapid deforestation, over-fishing, coastal erosion and tourism. Visiting those protected parks and areas sensibly might ensure their future preservation.

The Coast

As you need a 4WD to get to the exceptionally beautiful and peaceful Parque Nacional Monte Cristi (Monte Cristi National Park) (➤ 45) in the northwest, it's unlikely to ever become overcrowded. The park has pure white sands and dense mangroves. Here you may spot West Indian manatees (*Trichechus manatus*), also known as sea cows. They feed on sea grasses, pulling out and carrying the vegetation between their flippers.

National Parks and Gardens

The largest of the country's 16 national parks is the dry desert Parque Nacional Jaragua (Jaragua National Park) which boasts a huge flock of flamingos and over 50 per cent of the country's bird species. Parque Nacional Los Haïtises (Los Haïtises National Park) (➤ 45) is a favourite for short safaris. Parque Nacional del Este (➤ 59) encompasses the jewel of Isla Saona (Saona Island) (➤ 16, 60). For most, it's best to book an organised tour as the parks have few services, although this wildness appeals to independent travellers. The Jardín Botánico Nacional Rafael Moscoso (National Botanic Gardens), near Santo Domingo, is one of the largest in the Caribbean.

The Mountains

The Cordillera Central (➤ 14–15, 70) has Nepal-style vegetation, pine forests, mists and waterfalls. Active hikers can ascend Pico Duarte, the highest mountain in the Caribbean. Mule treks, run throughout the year, are a less strenuous option.

Bird life

The Dominican Republic shelters over 200 species of bird, including species and wintering birds from North America, as well as the Hispaniolan parrot, Hispaniolan woodpecker and Hispaniolan trogon.

Above: *the manatee, or sea cow, cruises along the ocean floor feeding on sea grass and marine plants*
Inset: *walking through the forests in the Cordillera Central, known as the Dominican Alps*

Dominican Republic's Famous

Sir Francis Drake
The visit in January 1586 by Sir Francis Drake is well recorded. On behalf of Queen Elizabeth I of England, Drake sailed for the New World and anchored his fleet of 25 ships off Santo Domingo. He marched his army into the city, burned buildings and demanded a ransom. You can see the chapel in which he slept at the Catedral Primada de América (➤ 29).

Cristobal Colón (Christopher Columbus)

Christopher Columbus, navigator and explorer, is recognised as having discovered the Americas for the Europeans. Born in 1451, Columbus gained much knowledge of geography through books such as the *Travels of Marco Polo*. King Ferdinand I and Queen Isabella of Spain gave the go-ahead to his first voyage, to discover the western route to the gold and jewel mines of Asia. He set off expecting to reach Japan, but following landings on San Salvador and Cuba, he arrived at modern-day Haiti in December 1492. On his second voyage he established the first settlement at what is now Parque Nacional La Isabela (La Isabela National Park, ➤ 19), where the foundations of Columbus's castle are preserved. Finding little gold on the island, Columbus was eventually recalled to Spain. He went on to discover Trinidad and explore Central America, but he retired as an ill and forgotten man. He died in 1506. Still the debate continues as to whether his remains are enshrined in the Faro a Colón (Columbus Lighthouse) in Santo Domingo, or under a monument in Seville Cathedral, Spain.

Right: *English seaman and explorer, Sir Francis Drake (c1540–96)*

Sammy Sosa

In 1924 the US Marines ended their eight-year occupation and left behind the legacy of baseball. Then along came Sammy Sosa. A former shoe-shine boy, Sosa would practise his catch using an empty juice container. He plays for Chicago Cubs and in 1998 broke a 37-year-old record for the number of home runs scored in a season. In 2000 Sosa won his second national league homer crown in three years.

Left: *a legend on the baseball field, Dominican-born Sammy Sosa*

Top Ten

Altos de Chavón 12
Bahía de Samaná 13
Cordillera Central 14–15
Isla Saona 16
Lago Enriquillo 17
Monumento a los Héroes, Santiago 18
Parque Nacional La Isabela 19
Playa Boca Chica 20
Puerto Plata 21
Zona Colonial, Santo Domingo 22

Above: *this tree on the north coast is believed to mark the spot where Columbus landed*
Right: *sculpture graces the entrance to the Museo de Arte Moderno in Santo Domingo*

1
Altos de Chavón

Frank Sinatra once performed at the amphitheatre

Stroll the cobbled streets and shop for paintings in this reconstructed medieval village perched high on cliffs above the Río Chavón.

- 25E2
- Near Casa de Campo Resort, La Romana
- 523 3333 (Casa de Campo Resort)
- Day and night
- French bakery and choice of bars, restaurants (££–£££)
- Self-drive, or *gua-gua* or taxi from La Romana
- Few
- Free
- Basílica de Nuestra Señora de la Altagracia (➤ 56); Isla Saona (➤ 16, 60)
- Regular music and concerts held

Altos de Chavón is open to everyone and demands at least half a day, or an evening. A replica 16th-century Mediterranean village complete with fountains and cobbled streets, it's more real than a movie set. It was built in 1976 by Dominican masons, carpenters and ironsmiths, under the direction of cinematographer Roberto Copa. Not simply a tourist attraction, the village is home to the School of Design where talented Dominicans and foreign students study art and design skills.

The highlight is a full-size Greek amphitheatre backed by 12 columns to represent the disciples of Christ. Frank Sinatra performed the first open-air concert here in 1982, followed by Julio Iglesias and Gloria Estefan. It's a bring-your-own-cushions event with tremendous acoustics. Around the village are quaint houses that are actually shops, complete with wooden shutters and clambering bougainvillea. There's a French bakery, restaurants, artists' studios, souvenirs and an expensive interior design store. By night the place is lit by lamps and is very romantic.

The Museo Arqueológico has objects from the Taino Indian period and documents the Colombian legacy. The Church of St Stanislaus, furnished with a statue of the Virgin Mary, is adorable. Locals swear that the singer Michael Jackson married Lisa Presley at its altar. During the evening the bars and classy gourmet restaurants, from Italian to French and Mexican, come alive.

2
Bahía de Samaná (Samana Bay)

A wild and dramatic peninsula visited annually by schools of magnificent humpback whales and a rare opportunity to see them close up.

On a map you can see how the 48km Península de Samaná forms the famous Bahía de Samaná (Samana Bay) where, from January to March, the humpback whales (*Megaptera novaeangliae*) congregate to breed and rear their new-born calves.

It's estimated that up to 5,000 humpback whales visit the coastline of the Dominican Republic after spending the summer months in the polar region feeding grounds. What sets them apart from other whales is the way they breach from the water. The whale heaves out of the ocean on its side, twists in the air and crashes its 40-tonnes of flesh back down in a memorable display. Huge flippers, almost a third of the body length and measuring up to 5m, are often the last to slip beneath the waves.

Fortunately for us, the humpback whale swims close to the coast. You can spot them either by standing on the shore at Banco de la Plata, north of Puerto Plata, or by hopping aboard a whale-watching cruise (➤ 54) into the Bahía de Samaná. Day trips can also drop you off on the popular offshore island of Cayo Levantado (➤ 42), known for its gorgeous beach and where the Bacardi television commercial was filmed. The town of Sánta Barbara de Samaná itself dates from the mid-1700s when families from the Canary Islands set up home here. It is backed by the mountains of the Cordillera Samaná.

- 25D3
- Península de Samaná
- Visitor information 538 2332
- Choice of bars, restaurants on the coast (££)
- Tour operators or bus from Santo Domingo and Puerto Plata
- Few
- Moderate–expensive
- If booking a tour, choose your operator carefully

Humpback whales, weighing up to 40 tonnes, visit the waters to the north of the Dominican Republic each winter

3
Cordillera Central (Dominican Alps)

Alpine air refreshes the tropical foothills of the Dominican Alps

Lush tropical forests and coffee plantations rise to the pine-clad backbone of the Dominican Republic and the highest peaks in the Caribbean.

24B3

Parque Nacional Armando Bermúdez/Parque Nacional José del Carmen Ramirez

National parks office 472 4204

Bars and restaurants in Jarabacoa (£–££)

Bus from Santo Domingo to Jarabacoa or tour operators: Iguana Mama 571 0908 or Caribe Tours 574 4796

Maxim Adventura, (➤ 85) offers trips

Free

Jarabacoa, Constanza (➤ 71)

Punching up through the heart of the country is the Cordillera Central, the 'Dominican Alps'. Connected to the Massif du Nord in Haiti, the range bends southwards until it meets the Caribbean coast and is the main watershed of the country. Visually, it's a world away from the beach. Walk or ride on horseback through forests to waterfalls or try rafting down the Río Yaque del Norte, the longest river in the country. See barefoot children astride mules fetching the daily water. It's a poor, simple life where locals scratch an existence from growing coconuts, bananas, avocados and coffee.

Over the past decade the Cordillera Central has attracted more visitors as the country pushes adventure tourism as an alternative to the beach holiday. Hundreds of walkers tackle the 48km ascent of Pico Duarte (3,175m), the highest peak, each year.

First climbed in 1944, the mountain bore the name Pico Trujillo after the country's ruthless dictator, Rafael Leonidas Trujillo, who added a few extra feet to its actual height in an elaborate boast. Following Trujillo's assassination in 1961, the mountain was renamed in honour of Juan Pablo Duarte, who fought for indepedence

in 1844. Almost anyone can have a go at trekking to Pico Duarte on a three-day, two-night trek. Or do it the easy way and ride a pack mule. It is spectacular, with a beauty to rival the high forests of Nepal. The alpine aroma is sweet. Temperatures drop low enough, however, for sweaters, and some people have even reported snowflakes falling on the summit.

Farther south, in the Valle Nuevo, only the fit attempt the trek through an unspoiled forest. It involves days of walking and you need plenty of stamina.

The thunderous roar of the Salto de Jimenoa waterfall is a highlight of a trip to the Dominican Alps

4

Isla Saona (Saona Island)

Daytrippers arrive at Isla Saona, a jewel in the Parque Nacional del Este

Reached only by boat, the island boasts pristine, white beaches shaded with swinging palms and a shallow sea of blue and green hues.

- 25F2
- Parque Nacional del Este, La Altagracia province
- National parks office 472 4204
- Take a picnic, or book through an operator (lunch is included)
- From La Romana or Bayahibe
- Few
- Moderate price, included in boat tour
- Altos de Chavón (➤ 12)
- See also ➤ 60

Isla Saona is a jewel in the Parque Nacional del Este (➤ 59), a trapezoid at the far southeastern tip of the country. The park itself is known for its beauty and impressive caves with pre-Columbian petroglyphs and pictographs. Sightings of iguanas, dolphins and turtles are common.

Saona was discovered by Christopher Columbus and is believed to be named after Sabona in Italy. It is the only inhabited place in the park. Reached only by speedboat or catamaran, the island is a popular, full-day trip. In fact, it's a welcome relief to leave behind the sprawling resorts that appear to have eaten up the south coast. You speed past a shoreline of dry and sub-tropical humid forest still thick, considering that 60% of the coconuts were pulverised by Hurricane Georges in 1998. Starfish are magnified on the ocean floor and flying fish hover over the surface, racing with you, their fins flapping.

On a boat tour you usually arrive on the eastern side of Isla Saona, at a fishing village lined with pastel-coloured, palm-wood houses. Souvenirs and paintings are sold here. From the village it takes a few minutes in the boat to reach the main beach. The perfect white sands are clean and there are no ostentatious hotels. There are flush toilets but they are about all that's modern. Langoustines and lobsters sizzle on hot plates at open-air eateries run by the tour operators. All you do is eat, sleep and snorkel.

5

Lago Enriquillo (Lake Enriquillo)

Once crossed by the legendary Indian chief and now a perfect spot to photograph wild American crocodiles, iguanas and flocks of pink flamingos.

Shocking pink flamingos rise above Lago Enriquillo

Lago Enriquillo is a remnant of an ancient channel that united the Bay of Neiba in the Dominican Republic with the Bay of Port-au-Prince in Haiti. The lake is an inland saltwater sheet of tea-stain-coloured water and it lies 40m below sea level, the lowest point in the Caribbean. Over 300 American crocodiles live here.

The lake is named after the Cacique Enriquillo, an Indian chief who fought for freedom against the Spaniards in this area. He utilised the island within the lake, Isla Cabritos (➤ 65), as his retreat. No human lives here nowadays, but there are plenty of iguanas, the two species known as *rinoceros* and *ricordi*. The iguanas and crocodiles are both considered endangered and hunting is illegal.

You can take a tour just to the shores of the lake. Here you'll definitely see iguanas. Because visitors have fed them, they are now so tame that they come running up to you like puppies. Groove lines in the sand indicate the drag of their tails. To see the crocodiles means a boat trip (➤ 68) across the lake to disembark at a small wooden jetty on Isla de Cabritos. Then it's a 2.5km walk through a corridor of cacti to a beach made from minute shells. Go silently and you'll see crocodiles sunning on the banks, their mouths open to ventilate. As soon as they detect you they slide into the lake and swim away. The finale of the crocodile trip is a glide past pink flamingos before they take off en masse in amazing flight.

- 24A2
- Parque Nacional Isla Cabritos
- National parks office 472 4204
- Daily – permit required
- Drinks and snacks on site (£)
- By tour operator or taxi from Baharona
- None
- Moderate
- Isla Cabritos (➤ 65); Baharona (➤ 65)

6

Monumento a los Héroes (Heroes' Monument), Santiago

24C4

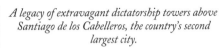

Santiago de los Caballeros

Visitor information 582 5885

8–5 (Closed for repair, due to re-open in 2003)

Choice of fast-food bars and steak restaurants at the foot (£–££)

Express bus from Santo Domingo or Puerto Plata

None Cheap

The monument to the nation's heroes towers over Santiago

A legacy of extravagant dictatorship towers above Santiago de los Cabelleros, the country's second largest city.

This eight-storey, 67m-high, white marble building is a monument to the nation's heroes of independence. To give it its full title, Monumento a los Héroes de la Restauración de la República pokes above the rooftops of the city known simply as Santiago. Built by Rafael Leonidas Trujillo, the egotistical dictator who ruled the country ruthlessly from 1930 to 1961, it is either grotesque or impressive – you decide. Trujillo had the habit of erecting monuments and busts in worship of himself wherever he found space.

Ornate, trimmed trees and national flags surround the bottom. Steps lead to the base, a cubic, mausoleum-style structure that rises to what resembles a screwdriver pointing upwards. Some say the figure at the top of the monument, which appears to be holding up the sky, was meant to be Trujillo. Inside, you can take the lift or climb exhausting flights of stairs to the top, remembering your camera for the magnificent panoramic views of Santiago, bordered by mountains of the fertile Cibao Valley. At the top of the staircase are works by Spanish painter Vela Zanetti.

At sunset, watch the sun sink behind the mountains and the dust from the city streets puff up like clouds. Someone might try to sell you a rose, or potato chips. A bride and groom might be having their wedding photographs taken. On 26 February, the day before the Independence Day celebrations, entire families gather together here. The children are dressed in colourful costumes speckled with tiny bells, and they wear carnival masks.

7

Parque Nacional La Isabela (La Isabela National Park)

The foundations of Columbus's first New World teeter at the edge of the Atlantic, where archaeologists are still making discoveries.

Remembering the days of Columbus's rule in the museum at the Parque Nacional La Isabela

Christopher Columbus brought the Spanish language to the Dominican Republic. He was blown to the island he named *La Isla Española* accidentally, by trade winds. Columbus originally landed in Haiti, in December 1492. There he ordered that the wrecked timber from his ship, *Santa María*, be used to build a fort called Puerta de la Navidad (Port Christmas). On his return voyage Columbus discovered the fort had been burned and his men massacred. He then founded La Isabela in honour of the Spanish queen. The area was divided into five territories, each headed by a Taino Indian chief. The Indians used stone cooking implements and were skilled at creating ceramics and carving images of their own gods from mahogany. The Spaniards enlisted the Indians to dig for gold but due to disease or fighting both natives and colonists began to die. You can see some of their graves, although the white crosses are not authentic.

In the Parque Nacional La Isabela (La Isabela National Park) a fraction of the walls of Columbus's castle are visible, as are the foundations of the first church of the New World and the fortress. It's difficult to distinguish what is original and what was rebuilt for the 500th anniversary celebrations of Colombus's discovery. A museum displays Indian artefacts, from necklaces to carvings of turtle shells and arrowheads. There's a drawing of Columbus, a model of the *Santa María* and, outside, a reconstructed Taino Indian settlement.

- 24B4
- Bay of La Isabela, south of El Castillo town
- National parks office 472 4204/571 8575
- 8–5
- Choice near by (£–££)
- Best reached by tour or self-drive
- Good
- Modest admission fee
- Puerto Plata (➤ 21, 50) Parque Nacional Monte Cristi (➤ 45)
- Celestino Torres offers guided tours and speaks a little English

8

Playa Boca Chica

Tourists and locals relax on the vast beach of Boca Chica

Flat sands blend into a smooth, shallow lagoon protected by a reef at this favourite haunt for holidaymakers and locals alike.

25D2

Boca Chica, near Santo Domingo

Visitor information 523 5106

Day and night

Good choice of bars, restaurants (£–££)

Express bus from Parque Central, Santo Domingo or *gua-gua*

None

Free

Santo Domingo (➤ 26)

'Boca chica' means 'little mouth' and Playa Boca Chica's beach is shaped like a bay. Said to be the Caribbean's largest natural swimming pool, the mirror-like stretch of water has no crashing surf and is an effortless place to swim. For Santo Domingans it's their local beach, and you'll see many splashing around among the tourists. Families with children wade out to a small island and, aside from swimming, go yachting, snorkelling, scuba diving or riding the banana boat until they fall off, laughing hysterically. At the main entrance to the beach are wooden shacks selling fried fish and pizza-size rounds of batter called *yani queque*.

The resort thrived as a rich Dominicans' getaway during the years of dictator Trujillo. From the 1960s it pulled in jetsetters from all over the world until new resorts lured them away. Today Boca Chica is still busy but it's by no means glitzy. A problem of prostitution has led to the creation of tourist police who round up the young girls and boys periodically. Behind the beach is a narrow, winding tourist street lined with souvenir shops, bars and lobster restaurants. At night the street is closed to traffic and restaurant chairs and tables spill out into the centre.

Neptuno's Restaurant is blessed with a most romantic setting. A wooden walkway leads out across the still waters to a replica of Christopher Columbus's ship, *Santa María*, which you can board. The walkway has glass panels revealing coral gardens and darting fish. The prospect is serene when the candelight flickers and the moon is full.

9
Puerto Plata

The place Columbus named the 'port of silver' and its statue-crowned peak gives you cigars, amber jewellery and shopping bargains galore.

Those that make the effort to visit Puerto Plata (► 50), the largest town on the north coast, are in for a treat. It's easily explored on foot. The pretty square of Parque Luperón is the focal point, surrounded by pastel-painted 19th-century architecture and the art deco-style Catholic Church of San Felipe. Sit in the square beside the central pavilion and listen as the clock tower passes the time. On Sunday mornings you'll hear harmonious celebrations at the white-painted church on the corner. The *malecón* (seafront promenade) comes alive at festival time. You can't miss the brass statue of General Gregorio Luperón, pointing towards the city. He fought against the Spanish in the mid-1800s and, when in power, briefly made Puerto Plata the republic's capital.

Puerto Plata is so called because Columbus either thought the harbour shimmered like a silver plate or the backdrop of mountains shone like the precious metal. He introduced sugarcane, which became as important as the port's trade in tobacco and cattle hides. The port was abandoned when its economy was undermined by locals trading with enemy pirate fleets. The fort, bristling with cannons, was built at the mouth of the bay to ward off pirates. It's well-preserved and ringed with a grassy bank.

- 24C4
- Puerto Plata
- Visitor information 586 3676
- Good choice of cafés and restaurants (£–££)
- Express bus from Santo Domingo, *gua-gua* or taxi from north coast
- Few
- Santiago (► 18, ► 52), Playa Dorada (► 47), Museo del Ambar Dominicano (► 43), Fuerte de San Felipe (► 42)

Puerto Plata is a charming colonial town of gingerbread-style houses and boutiques

10

Zona Colonial, Santo Domingo

Watch cigars being rolled and then buy, at the cigar shop in Parque Colón

First European city in the New World and seat of Spanish power, this historic gathering of architecture and treasures is now world renowned.

33A2

Santo Domingo

Excellent choice of cafés, bistros and restaurants (££–£££)

Express buses from major towns

Few

Free or cheap–moderate

Faro a Colón (➤ 30–31); Museo del Hombre Dominicano (➤ 35)

Tourist office, 103 Calle Isabel la Católica, Parque Colón, 9–5 daily, 686 3858

It's easy to see why Zona Colonial, in the capital of Santo Domingo, was declared a World Heritage Site by UNESCO in 1990. Once ruled by Spain in the days of pirates, galleons and gold, its late-Gothic style architecture bears a hint of Renaissance and years of wear are traceable on rusty cannons. See how the people lived at that time at the home of Columbus's son, Diego, now the Museo Alcázar de Colón (➤ 32, 34). The Catedral Basílica Menor de Santa Marie, Primada de América (➤ 28–29), with its early motifs of Catholicism, is claimed by Dominicans to be the first cathedral of the Americas. Cobbled Las Damas street is said to be the first street. Then there's the first university, the first hospital... the list goes on.

Splendid though it is, Santo Domingo was built in 1498 with enormous cost to the lives of native Indian and African slaves. Columbus's brother, Bartolomé, built it like a fortress on the eastern side of the Río Ozama to protect the people from pirates. After being destroyed by a hurricane it was moved to its present site.

So contained in a grid is Zona Colonial that all its sites can be seen in a full day's stroll (but take longer if you're really keen). Tour groups fail to do it justice. To absorb the atmosphere and understand a smattering of colonial history, it's best to stay overnight, sip cappuccino and eat well at the old city's fine cafés, bistros and restaurants.

What to See

Santo Domingo	26–37
In the Know	38–39
North & North Coast	41–55
Food and Drink	48–49
Southeast	56–63
Southwest	64–9
Cordillera Central	70–72

Above: *souvenirs they'll love back home*
Right: *the national flag*

ESCUEL
DE

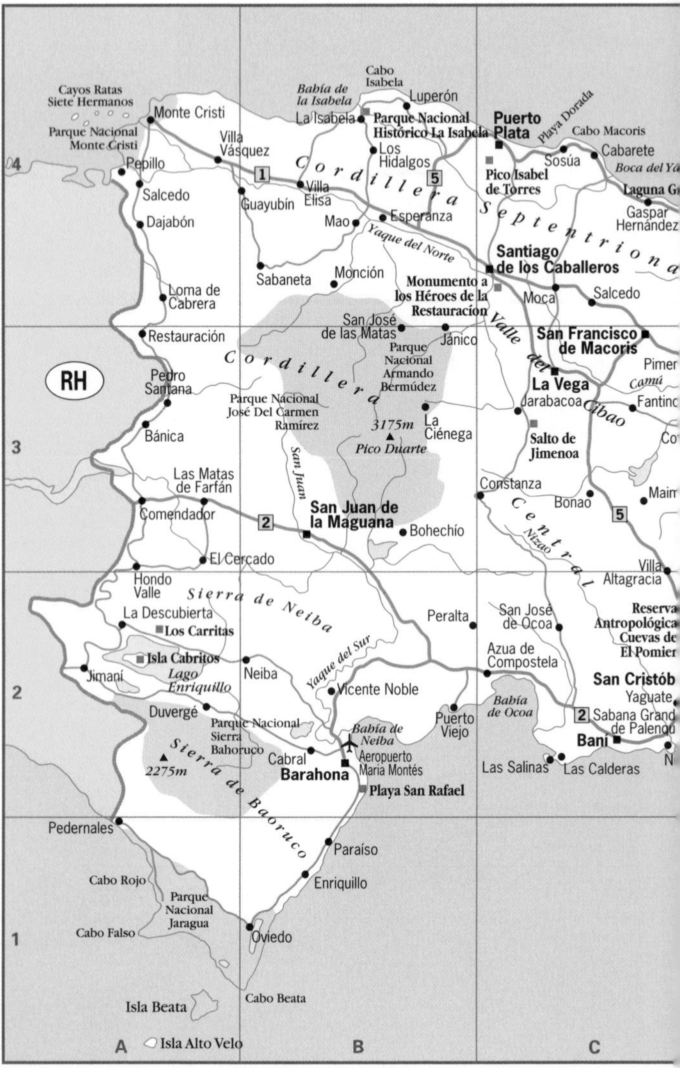
Cayos Ratas
Siete Hermanos
Parque Nacional Monte Cristi
Monte Cristi
Villa Vásquez
Pepillo
Salcedo
Dajabón
Guayubín
Villa Elisa
Mao
Esperanza
Sabaneta
Monción
Loma de Cabrera
Restauración
Pedro Santana
Bánica
RH
Cabo Isabela
Bahía de la Isabela
La Isabela
Luperón
Parque Nacional Histórico La Isabela
Los Hidalgos
Puerto Plata
Playa Dorada
Cabo Macoris
Sosúa
Cabarete
Boca del Ya
Pico Isabel de Torres
Laguna G
Gaspar Hernández
Cordillera Septentrional
Yaque del Norte
Santiago de los Caballeros
Monumento a los Héroes de la Restauracíon
Moca
Salcedo
San José de las Matas
Jánico
San Francisco de Macoris
Valle del Cibao
Parque Nacional Armando Bermúdez
La Vega
Pimer
Camú
Jarabacoa
Fantino
Cordillera
Parque Nacional José Del Carmen Ramírez
La Ciénega
3175m
Pico Duarte
Salto de Jimenoa
Co
San Juan
Las Matas de Farfán
Comendador
Constanza
Bonao
Maim
Cordillera Central
Nizao
San Juan de la Maguana
Bohechío
El Cercado
Villa Altagracia
Hondo Valle
Sierra de Neiba
La Descubierta
Los Carritas
Isla Cabritos
Lago Enriquillo
Jimaní
Neiba
Yaque del Sur
Peralta
San José de Ocoa
Reserva Antropológica Cuevas de El Pomier
Azua de Compostela
San Cristób
Yaguate
Vicente Noble
Duvergé
Parque Nacional Sierra Bahoruco
Bahía de Neiba
Puerto Viejo
Bahía de Ocoa
Sabana Grand de Palenqu
Baní
Sierra de Baoruco
2275m
Cabral
Barahona
Aeropuerto Maria Montés
Playa San Rafael
Las Salinas
Las Calderas
Pedernales
Paraíso
Enriquillo
Cabo Rojo
Parque Nacional Jaragua
Cabo Falso
Oviedo
Isla Beata
Cabo Beata
Isla Alto Velo
1
2
5
A
B
C
1
2
3
4

RH Haiti

ESCUEL
DE

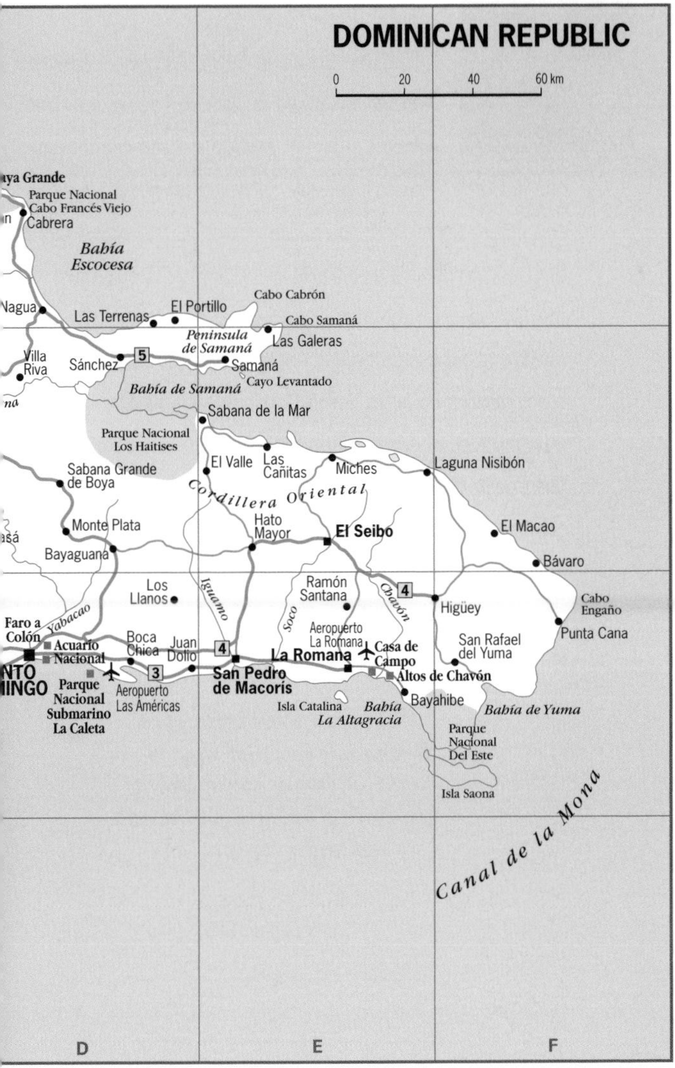
DOMINICAN REPUBLIC
0 20 40 60 km
ya Grande
Parque Nacional Cabo Francés Viejo
Cabrera
Bahía Escocesa
Nagua
Las Terrenas
El Portillo
Cabo Cabrón
Cabo Samaná
Península de Samaná
Las Galeras
Villa Riva
Sánchez
5
Samaná
Cayo Levantado
Bahía de Samaná
Sabana de la Mar
Parque Nacional Los Haitises
Sabana Grande de Boya
El Valle
Las Cañitas
Miches
Laguna Nisibón
Cordillera Oriental
Monte Plata
Hato Mayor
El Seibo
El Macao
Bayaguana
Bávaro
Los Llanos
Iguamo
Ramón Santana
Chavón
4
Higüey
Cabo Engaño
Soco
Yabacao
Faro a Colón
Acuario Nacional
Boca Chica
Juan Dolio
Aeropuerto La Romana
La Romana
Casa de Campo
San Rafael del Yuma
Punta Cana
NTO
INGO
3
San Pedro de Macorís
Altos de Chavón
Parque Nacional Submarino La Caleta
Aeropuerto Las Américas
Isla Catalina
Bahía La Altagracia
Bayahibe
Bahía de Yuma
Parque Nacional Del Este
Isla Saona
Canal de la Mona
D
E
F

Santo Domingo

It could be Seville in Spain. Alleyways are lined with whitewashed or painted houses and black wrought iron for windows. Catholic churches rise in Gothic/Renaissance style, while *merengue* plays in bars and cafés. Santo Domingo's Zona Colonial, the oldest city in the New World, is a throwback to the days of Spanish rule. On the flip side is a modern, financial city and port of shopping malls, and the site of the Pan American Games 2003.

Many visitors come to Santo Domingo for a whistle-stop tour of a few historic sites, grab a few souvenirs and bargains then head back to their resort or hotel. It's a shame, because the capital, first city of the New World, is infused with history, music, art, crafts and excellent cuisine. The hotchpotch of the country's Spanish and African ancestry bubbles here in a mix of architecture and wealth. It's a buzzing, vibrant city.

> *'Cerveza Presidente, Ron Bermudez; beer and rum; rum and beer. Never saw anything like it, a veritable capital spread out under the sun...'*
>
> MAURICE LEMOINE
> *Bitter Sugar*, 1985

Santo Domingo

Above: *ruined but not forgotten, the first hospital of the Americas is found down a side street in the Zona Colonial*

Originally called Nueva Isabela, Santo Domingo was founded in 1498 by Columbus's brother, Bartolomé, on the eastern bank of the river, Río Ozama. Destroyed by a hurricane, the city was moved in 1502 to its present site and governed by Columbus's son, Diego. The name is thought to be derived from the 12th-century teaching apostle, Santo Domingo de Guzman, inventor of the rosary. During his dictatorship Trujillo renamed the capital Ciudad Trujillo in honour of himself, although it reverted back to Santo Domingo after his assassination in 1961.

Numerous hurricanes have left their mark so what you see is a mix of layers and add-ons, with some old colonial buildings restored by well-known hotel groups. For daytrippers there are shops, boutiques, an immaculate botanic garden, art galleries, museums and an aquarium. A new swing bridge across the river takes you to the east, to a monument (said to contain the remains of Columbus), the aquarium and beaches enjoyed by the locals.

Time your visit to Santo Domingo on Independence Day, 27 February (or the last Sunday in February – check beforehand) to witness either the patriotism of the Dominican rulers or their extended egos. The nation's fighting force – troops, commandos, marines and the police riot squad – stand to attention in the blistering heat. They then march past the president and his generals on the main ocean front artery, Avenue George Washington. The parade ends with a posse of big guns, tanks and fighter planes before four parachutists landed at the president's feet.

Below: *shoeshine boys work for a few pesos near the cathedral in Parque Colón*

What to See in Santo Domingo

25D2
Av 28 de Enero
766 1709 (office hours Mon–Fri)
Tue–Sun 9:30–6
Kiosk serving drinks (£)
Few
Cheap

ACUARÍO NACIONAL ✪

The National Aquarium has an attractive landscaped setting alongside the blue of the Caribbean Sea. The marine animals and fish themselves are housed in tanks and scores of families are attracted to this, the largest aquarium in the Caribbean. You'll see plenty of sharks and turtles and the colourful fish and crustaceans (crabs, shrimps etc) commonly found in Dominican waters.

33A2
Parque Independencia, Zona Colonial
Daily
Along El Conde street (£–££)
None
Free

ALTAR DE LA PATRIA ✪✪

The pedestrianised El Conde shopping street runs from Parque Colón to the 17th-century gate of Puerte El Conde. As you pass under the archway, the white mausoleum, Altar de la Patria (Altar of the Nation), confronts you. Inside are the remains of the three heroes of independence: Juan Pablo Duarte, Francisco del Rosario Sánchez and Ramón Matías Mella. An eternal flame burns in a crypt below.

33A2
Parque Colón, Zona Colonial
Daily 9–4
Cafés in Parque Colón and El Conde Street (£–££)
Few
Free
Dress appropriately, shorts and vests not allowed

CATEDRAL BASÍLICA MENOR DE SANTA MARIE, PRIMADA DE AMÉRICA ✪✪✪

On the north side of the Parque Colón stands the most important monument in the Dominican Republic, the Catedral Basílica Menor de Santa Marie, Primada de América (first cathedral of the Americas); it is a beauty you should not miss. In the early 1500s Diego Columbus, Christopher's son, laid the first stone where a wooden church once stood. Construction took around 40 years, but the sculptor died before it was finished. This explains the lack

of a proper bell tower and the mixture of architectural styles – a commanding blend of Gothic, Romanesque and baroque. Inside, under a magnificent vaulted ceiling are 14 different chapels. Francis Drake sacked much of the cathedral and even slept in the Capilla de Santa Ana. It is believed that the sarcophagus containing the remains of Columbus was found here during restoration work in 1877. In 1992 the remains were moved for the 500th anniversary of Columbus's landing, to the Faro a Colón (► 30–31).

Columbus's son laid the first stone on the site of what is reputedly the first cathedral in the Americas

FARO A COLÓN

✪✪✪

- 25D2
- Parque Mirador del Este
- 592 5217
- Daily 10–5
- Few
- Cheap

Perhaps because of its out-of-the-way location, across the Río Ozamo, the Faro a Colón (Lighthouse to Columbus) doesn't attract the number of visitors once expected to put its 100 washrooms to use. Many simply circle the colossal concrete and white marble, recumbent cross in a tour bus, photographing it through the ornamental trees and ponds. It is a must to stop and look inside this blatant result of President Balaguer's extravagance. Built to house the supposed remains of Christopher Columbus, the lighthouse cost US$200million. Its trademark is a string of rooftop lasers which project an image of a cross, visible for miles, onto the night sky. The winner of an architectural contest to design the monument was a British man, Joseph Gleve. He only managed to see the base being made because dictator Trujillo stopped construction, probably for economic reasons. Gleve died in 1965 and another designer worked on the monument until it was completed in 1991, ready for the celebration of the 500th

A marine stands guard at the tomb of Faro a Colón reputedly containing the remains of Christopher Columbus

anniversary of Columbus's landing. First, you climb steps to an entrance decorated by marble tablets inscribed with quotations about exploration from the New Testament and from Greek philosophers. An alleyway down the centre of the cross is flanked by mahogany doors, behind which are displays of artefacts representative of 65 countries. The marble mausoleum, purportedly containing the remains of Christopher Columbus, is decorated with bronze and gold. Originally housed in the cathedral (➤ 28–29) the structure was dismantled into hundreds of pieces and reassembled at its present site. The lighthouse is designed in such a way that the tomb is protected from hurricanes and earthquakes.

Overlooking the fortress of Santo Domingo on the banks of the Río Ozama

FORTALEZA OZAMA ✪✪✪

Fortaleza Ozama (Fortress of Santo Domingo) is considered the oldest of its type in the Americas. It was built from 1505 by Governor Nicolás de Ovando when the city was moved to this side of the river. An elaborate gateway welcomes you into an expanse of trim, green lawn stretching to the Torre del Homenaje (Tower of Homage). The tower resembles a medieval castle, with turrets and battlements. During the many occupations of the country, the Spanish, French, Haitians and Americans flew their flag atop its battlements. Staircases lead to the top and to a grand view of the river and its traffic. In the grounds is a bronze statue of Gonzalo Fernández de Oviedo. Other details to look out for around the fort are cannons pointing out across the river, coats of arms, the arsenal and the old army barracks.

- 33B2
- Calle de las Damas, Zona Colonial
- 685 8532
- Tue–Sat 9–7, Sun 10–3
- Good choice nearby (£–££)
- None
- Cheap
- Guided tours available

Zona Colonial

Distance
3km

Time
Half a day with lunch, longer with shopping and rest stops. To see all the sites takes more than a day

Start/end point
Parque Colón, Zona Colonial
33A2

Lunch
Choice of restaurants at Plaza La Hispanidad (£–££)

This tour begins with the Catedral Primada de América (► 28–29) and Parque Colón (► 37) before exploring highlights of the old city.

Head along El Conde Street and turn right at Calle Hostos.

At No 215 is Soto Galeria, an antiques house with Cuban paintings, and English and local objects and furniture.

Walk further, passing painted colonial buildings with wrought ironwork for windows.

The pink building, now the Italian Embassy, offers Dominicans Italian language and painting classes. Browse round the Ruinas del Hospital San Nicolás de Bari (► 37).

Walk uphill, passing wooden houses on your left.

The houses survived a hurricane in the 1930s. Immediately ahead are the ruins of the first monastery, Monasterio de San Francisco where, nowadays, Dominicans can marry.

On the historic threshold of the first monastery of the Americas in the Zona Colonial

Turn downhill to busy Calle Arzobispo Meriño. Turn left and to the Museo Mundo de Ambar (► 36) on your left. Turn right out of the museum, cross the road and turn immediately left downhill and right into Plaza de la Hispanidad.

Explore the Museo Alcázar de Colón (► 34).

Walk alongside the river to Museo de las Casas Reales (► 35) on the right. Keep straight ahead, following Calle Las Damas, passing the Panteón Nacional (► 37) on the right, gift shops and the French Embassy. Eventually a side street on the left leads to the archway of the Fortaleza Ozama (► 31). Explore the fortress and battlements. Head back out of the archway and up Calle Pellerano Alfau until you face the cathedral and Parque Colón to the right.

A typical house front in the Zona Colonial

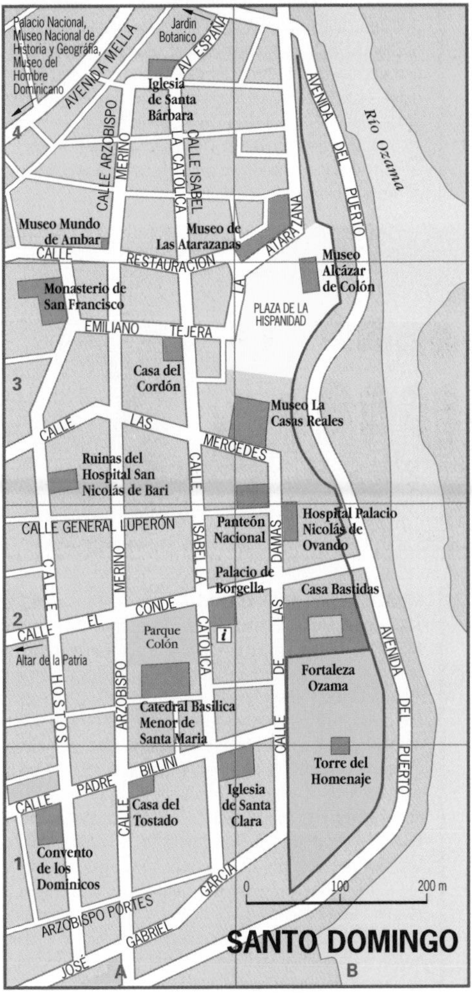

33B3
Calle Las Damas, Zona Colonial
689 5946
Tue–Sun 9–12, 3–6
Cafés and restaurants opposite (£–££)
Few
Cheap
English-speaking guides offer tours

MUSEO ALCÁZAR DE COLÓN

Diego Columbus's palace and Spanish seat of government is now the Museo Alcázar de Colón (House of Columbus). It was built by 300 Indian slaves from 1511 to 1516. Diego lived here with his wife, Doña María de Toledo, until 1523, when they returned to Spain. Here many expeditions to conquer more of the Americas were planned. Alcázar is an Arabic word and Moorish influences on the decorated beamed ceilings of the interior are noticeable. Carved mahogany details and candle holders sporting grotesque faces are said to ward off evil spirits. Few pieces of furniture are originals, though many are representative of that period or slightly later. Of particular interest is a replica of Diego's mahogany and gold-leaf bed, a writing bureau, a bed engraved with the Columbus family crest and a trunk made from African elephant hide. The English-speaking guide insists that the testament signed by Queen Isabella of Spain, giving power to Diego, is the real thing. The balcony overlooks the Plaza de la Hispanidad and the ruins of the Monasterio de San Francisco.

Below: *Museo Alcázar de Colón displays its Moorish influences*

33B4
Calle Colón No 4 La Atarazana, Zona Colonial
682 5834
Daily 9–5
Cafés and restaurants nearby (£–££)
Good
Cheap

MUSEO DE LAS ATARAZANAS

The atmospheric Museo de las Atarazanas (Shipyard or Maritime Museum) is housed in a former warehouse facing east over the Río Ozama. This brilliant maritime archaeological museum recounts life on a Spanish galleon for crew and passengers in the 17th century. More enthralling is the tale of the *Concepción*, part of the New World fleet which sank during a hurricane in 1641 on its way back to Spain. An expedition in 1686 did recover some silver and bullion. Nearly 300 years later, in 1976, Burt Webber and Jack Hoskins found 13 wrecks but not the *Concepción*. In 1978 a second, better equipped, expedition finally found the galleon, with a hoard of treasure undiscovered in the bow and stern. The museum has photographs of the salvage team at work. Some of the hoard is on display with descriptions in English, including animal bones, an ear wax remover and pieces-of-eight.

MUSEO DE LAS CASAS REALES ✪✪

The Museo La Casas Reales (Museum of the Royal Houses) occupies what was the 16th palace of the Spanish Governor's Royal Court. To its side is Calle Las Damas, the cobbled street of the ladies and the first street in the Americas. Nearly all the information signs in this brilliant museum are in Spanish, but you can hire a guide inside for a small fee. Very spacious, its grand rooms are tastefully arranged with earthenware, maps, treasures from sunken galleons, furniture and paintings, an armoury section and a wonderful apothecary, set out like a cook's kitchen. Outside is a sundial, which enabled the judges seated in the court to tell the time.

- 33B3
- Calle Las Damas, Zona Colonial
- 682 4204
- Daily 9–5
- Cafés and restaurants nearby (£–££)
- Good
- Moderate

MUSEO DEL HOMBRE DOMINICANO ✪✪✪

Although big and off-putting, the Museo del Hombre Dominicano (Museum of the Dominican Man) is actually just two floors of exhibitions, but definitely worth a visit. It begins with finds from archaeological digs that predate the Taino Indians, as far back as 3000 BC. An excellent collection of Taino artefacts hails from the north and east of the country. Most of the items were unearthed in a massive site near Boca Chica, and are important because of their variety and condition. To archaeologists the site is considered the jewel of the Antilles. A former director of the museum, Professor Dato Pagán Perdomo, was an authority on Indian rock art and has written many books on findings from his own expeditions. A glass cabinet contains skeletons of Tainos, resting in the foetal position as they believed in reincarnation. They crafted images of their gods from stone. The one with a crescent-shaped head is the God of the Moon, though the principal god was Trigonolito, a triangular image. Moving upwards, the museum deals with the actions of the Spanish conquistadors and the culture, Catholicism and cockfighting they introduced. Information boards are in Spanish, but an English- and French-speaking guide is available to hire.

- 33A4
- Plaza de la Cultura
- 687 3622
- Tue–Sun 10–5
- Good
- Cheap

Above: *treasures from Spanish galleons and more on show at the Museo de las Casas Reales*

A worker turns raw amber into delicate jewellery at the amber museum

- 33A4
- Calle Arzobispo Meriño 462, Zona Colonial
- 682 3309
- Mon–Sat 8:30–6, Sun 9–1
- Cafés and restaurants nearby (£–££)
- Few
- Cheap

MUSEO MUNDO DE AMBAR

Santo Domingo's Museo Mundo de Ambar (Amber Museum) has a tremendous collection of Dominican amber and examples of amber from around the world. Pieces are for sale in the souvenir and jewellery shop downstairs. Look out for the fossilised butterfly in one fragment and an absolutely exquisite carved Taino god. Explanations are in English and there are also guided tours. At the back of the shop is an open workroom where craftsmen let you watch them fashion beads from the amber. The rare larimar stone is also on show.

- 33A4
- Plaza de la Cultura
- 686 6668
- Tue–Sun 10–5
- Good
- Cheap

MUSEO NACIONAL DE HISTORIA Y GEOGRÁFIA

In the newer part of Santo Domingo is Plaza de la Cultura, featuring the national theatre fronted by a statue of Giuseppe Verdi. Nearby is a modern art gallery and a crop of museums. Museo Nacional de Historia y Geográfia (National History and Geography Museum) has a car, punctured with eight bullet holes. Its boot is where the body of dictator Trujillo was bundled following his assassination in 1961. An assortment of objects are connected with the Trujillo terror era, including his death mask and a replica of an electric chair. What's so chilling is the copy of a real photograph taken whilst one poor man was being electrocuted.

- 33A4
- Av. México
- 695 800/689 3434
- VIP tours by appointment
- Few
- Free

PALACIO NACIONAL

The Palacio Nacional (National Palace) was built from marble in 1947 on Trujillo's instructions, as a pale, mandarin-coloured replica of the White House in Washington DC. Seat of the country's government, it is massive, bordered by wrought-iron railings, and is guarded by the military. It stands opposite the Ministry of Tourism in an area of the city known as Gazcue. You'll see many wealthy houses with fancy balconies, mainly because Trujillo drew in many important white immigrants, among whom some were architects. Nowadays those with money are tempted to the outskirts of the city, away from the traffic.

PANTEÓN NACIONAL ✪✪✪

The Panteón Nacional (National Pantheon) was originally a Jesuit church, built from 1714 to 1748. It was restored and renamed by Trujillo in 1958 to celebrate an international fair. Inside are the tombs of heroes of the independence struggle. Above and in front of the altar hangs a chandelier, a present from General Franco of Spain. Above the pews are what the guide tells you are iron screens bearing the swastika sign, a gift from Adolf Hitler of Germany. A flame for the heroes is forever lit at the foot of the altar. The best time to be here is at noon, when the national anthem is played and there's a changing of the guard.

- 33B2
- Calle de las Damas, Zona Colonial
- Tue–Sun 8–6, Mon 2–6
- Good choice nearby (£–££)
- Few
- Free

PARQUE COLÓN ✪✪✪

Parque Colón (Columbus Park) is a bustling square of shoe-shine boys, pavement sweepers and workers grabbing a quick coffee. It has a cigar shop with a mobile hut which offers prospective buyers a free smoke under the nearby fig tree. Loved by the pigeons, the bronze statue of Columbus, sculpted by Ernesto Gilbert, a French sculptor, was built in 1887 as a present from France. Some say Columbus's left hand points north to La Isabela (➤ 19), the first settlement of the New World, others say to Asia, his intended destination. His right hand rests on a compass and a map. At each corner is a ship's masthead, symbolising his four voyages to the Americas. Inscribing the column with the Admiral's name is Queen Anna Caona, wife of Indian chief Enriquillo, who had the courage to revolt against the Spaniards. Adjacent to the park are the Palacio de Borgellá (the presidential palace of the Haitian governors from 1822 to 1844), which now houses the tourism office, and the cathedral (➤ 28–29).

- 33A2
- Zona Colonial
- Cafés and restaurants (£–££)
- Good
- Tourist office: 103 Calle Isabel la Católica, 686 3858, Daily 9–5
- Cigar demonstrations Thu–Sun

Above: *tourists pause for a rest beneath the statue of Christopher Columbus in the Parque Colón*

RUINAS DEL HOSPITAL SAN NICOLÁS DE BARI ✪✪✪

The ruins of the first hospital in the Americas, the Ruinas del Hospital San Nicolás de Bari have not succumbed to restoration. Built from 1503, the hospital survived the plunders of Sir Francis Drake. Today pigeons inhabit its crumbled arches, walled on one side by mahogany trees.

- 33A3
- Calle Hostos, Zona Colonial
- Daily
- Plenty nearby (£–££)
- None
- Free

In the Know

If you only have a short time to visit the Dominican Republic and would like a flavour of the country, here are some ideas:

10 Ways to Be a Local

Learn a little Spanish – just a few words such as *buenos días*, (good morning). Away from holiday resorts, some phrases will be helpful.

Always greet everyone when entering a bar; Dominicans regard it as good manners. A nod will suffice, or a simple *buenos días*. When asking a question or for directions, greet the person first.

Sip some sugar cane juice if you wake up with a hangover

Learn to dance *merengue*, the national dance. You need only grasp a few steps before braving the dance floor.

Don't worry about tomorrow, because the Dominicans never do.

Take a long siesta. Shops and offices usually close for a couple of hours until 4PM.

Drink coconut juice from its shell, either from the bar or sold by the roadside for a few pesos.

Dine late and dance until dawn is how the Dominicans spend their evenings.

Dress smartly when entering a church, especially the cathedrals of Santo Domingo.

Smile a lot as the locals do.

Showing a dazzling smile this fruit vendor balances her wares

10 Good Places to Have Lunch

Restaurant Conde (£–£££) ✉ Parque Colón, Zona Colonial ☎ 682 6944. Corner brasserie with tables spilling out onto historic Parque Colón.

Pat'e Palo Brasserie (££) ✉ Atarazana 25, Zona Colonial ☎ 687 8089. Themed restaurant (the name means 'peg leg') with waiting staff dressed as pirates.

Restaurant La Carreta (£–££) ✉ 17 El Batey, Sosúa ☎ 571 1217. Italian serving fish soup, lobster, salads, pizzas, pastas, seafood.

Le Croissant de Paris (£) ✉ Cabarete. On the busy main street, serving breakfast and lunch – freshly baked pastries, ham croissants and coffee.

Hemingway's Café (£–££) ✉ Playa Dorada Plaza ☎ 320 2230. Fast food and live rock in this popular meeting place.

La Puntilla de Piergiorgo (£££) ✉ Sosúa ☎ 571 2215. Romantic setting perched above the ocean, serving excellent Italian food. Open all day.

Tipíco Bonao (££) ✉ Duarte Highway, between Santo Domingo and Santiago ☎ 248 7942 Seafood, chicken, lobster and international dishes.

Capitán Cook Restaurant (£–££) ✉ Playa El Cortecito, (Entrance Hoteles Fiesta y Carabela), Near Higüey ☎ 552 0645. Tables on the sand and a mouth-watering array of lobster, langoustine and octopus, washed down with sangria.

Neptuno's Restaurant (££–£££) ✉ Boca Chica ☎ 523 4703. Exquisite setting over a lagoon. Good fish and shellfish.

Restaurant El Rancho (££) ✉ Jarabacoa ☎ 574 4024/4557. In the foothills of the mountains. Fish, seafood, steaks, chicken, pizzas and sandwiches.

10 Top Activities

Stroll the beaches of Playa Dorada on the 'Amber Coast' (➤ 44).

Go on safari into the mountainous interior (➤ 72).

Shooting the rapids on the Río Yaque del Norte

Photograph waterfalls in the Dominican Alps, the Salto de Jimenoa at Jarabacoa being the most impressive (➤ 71).
Tour the Zona Colonial, the historic old city of the capital Santo Domingo (➤ 22, 32).
Go birdwatching in Parque Nacional Los Haïtses on an organised adventure tour.
Learn to windsurf at Cabarete, the world-famous championship resort (➤ 41).
Play golf at one of many courses, some offering superb landscaping and design.
Learn to scuba dive/snorkel with recognised diving schools, then book dives to the coral reefs and spectacular wrecks (➤ 85).
Watch baseball at the stadia in Santo Domingo.
Go rafting on the Río Yaque del Norte, the country's longest river.

10 Wildlife to Watch

Hispanolan parakeets flit around Parque Nacional Los Haïtses (➤ 45) and in the Cordillera Central (➤ 14–15, 70).
Manatees are spotted in the Parque Nacional del Este (➤ 59), around Isla Saona (➤ 16, 60), and at the Nacional Parque Monte Cristi (➤ 45).
Humpback whales visit the Península de Samaná each winter to calve (➤ 13, 54).
American crocodiles can be seen basking in the sun or lurking in the still waters of Lago Enriquillo (➤ 17, 68).
Iguanas are so tame on Isla Cabritos they run up to you expecting a titbit (➤ 65).
Dolphins frolic in the seas and oceans around the Dominican Republic.
Pink flamingos launch themselves from the shores of Lago Enriquillo (➤ 17, 68).
Sea lions make the audience laugh at Manatí Park (➤ 62).
Sea turtles crawl onto many patches of sand to lay their eggs. Also at the Acuarío Nacional in Santo Domingo (➤ 28).
American kestrels inhabit some of the the national parks but are hard to spot, they also perch on the top of telephone poles around Puerto Plata in the north (➤ 21).

10 Top Beaches

Cabarete: lively resort, famed for its windsurfing (➤ 41).
Sosúa: well-visited, as bustling as Cabarete (➤ 53).
Playa Dorada: the beach of **Puerto Plata**, a caramel curve of sand with rock pools where children can search for shrimps and crabs (➤ 47).
Playa Boca Chica: sheltered lagoon, ideal for children (➤ 20).
Punta Cana: the kind of soft, white sand beach known as paradise. Good watersports (➤ 63).
Cayo Levantado: setting of a Bacardi drinks television commercial (➤ 42).
Isla Saona: crystal waters, aquamarine colours and white, powdery sand (➤ 16, 60).
Bayahibe: a young person's hangout, busy with cruisers to Isla Saona. (➤ 57).
San Rafael: rugged, ungroomed and backed by green-clad hills and waterfalls.
Playa Grande: a northern watersports mecca (➤ 47).

Splashing around on the beaches of the southwest

Around the Country

From tropical rainforest and mountains to desert-dry savannah dotted with cacti, the natural landscape of the Dominican Republic is amazingly diverse. It's impossible, even during a 2-week stay, to see everything. Tours are plenty, though, and venturing outside your hotel complex or all-inclusive resort to explore or have lunch by the roadside means you'll be more in touch with the country and its people. The capital, Santo Domingo, is definitely worth a look, but if you can't make it, Puerto Plata and Santiago will whet your appetite. The cooler mountain air is a big draw, as are the national parks, lakes and forests, packed with wildlife and natural history, not forgetting some of the best beaches in the world.

'... there are in it [La Isla Española] many sierras and very high mountains, beyond comparison with the island of Tenerife, all very beautiful, of a thousand shapes, and all accessible and filled with trees of a thousand kinds and tall, seeming to touch the sky'

CHRISTOPHER COLUMBUS
on the island of Hispaniola, 1492

North and North Coast

In addition to its exquisite beaches and deep green national parks, the north has amber. The Dominican Republic is famous for its variety and clarity of amber and its astounding collection of fossils and jewellery. Found in the mountains between Puerto Plata and Santiago, amber is mined by hand, using picks and shovels. It is the fossilised sap from a type of carob tree that existed millions of years ago. Prized pieces contain fossilised insects and plants that became caught and embedded in the sticky, honey-like substance before it hardened. Also not found anywhere else in the world is larimar, a powder-blue stone believed to be either a variety of pectolite or a fossil. The biggest larimar mines are midway between Barahona and Baoruco.

Above: *sunbathers on Cabarete beach*
Below: *Haitian paintings create a vibrant montage at a market stall in Cabarete*

What to See in the North and Along the North Coast

CABARETE ✪✪

If you don't rise early enough to grab a sun lounger at lively Cabarete, then you could perch at a beach bar drinking cold Presidente beer to *merengue* tunes. This favourite holiday haunt is a windsurfing and kiteboarding centre – boards line up like dominoes on the beach. This is a good place to hire equipment and organise eco-tours, mountain bike trips and adventure safaris into the country's interior from the throng of adventure tour operators. Shop here, too, for sarongs, jewellery and Taino-style art. People read newspapers and take breakfast at French or German bakeries serving Belgian waffles. Shoeshine boys as young as eight offer to polish your shoes. Seafood restaurants and bars spill onto the beach. At night, happy hours and free spaghetti evenings take over. If you tire of Cabarete, then flit to nearby Sosúa and back in a *gua-gua*.

- 24C4
- Excellent choice (£–££)
- Visitor information 571 0962
- *Gua-gua* from Puerto Plata and Sosúa
- Gral G Luperón, Puerto Plata

The mid-16th century Fuerte de San Felipe guards the entrance to Puerto Plata

- 24C4
- Avenue Gregorio Luperón
- 586 2318
- Daily 8–5
- Good choice in Puerto Plata (£–££)
- None
- Gral G Luperón, Puerto Plata

FUERTE DE SAN FELIPE

The rounded walls of Fuerte de San Felipe (San Felipe Fort) once protected the Bahía de Puerto Plata, the port you can see in the background. Built by the Spaniards and completed in the 16th century, the fort was supposed to deter invasions from French buccaneers and other pirates, yet was never used in battle. Until the end of the Trujillo era in the 1960s, the fort served as a prison. Duarte, hero of independence, may have been held here. Deep within the fort's chambers is a scant collection of cannon and musket balls, and black-leaded fragments of 16th-century artillery. From its turrets you face the Atlantic, like the rusty cannons. A coral-bottomed moat, now empty, once had lethal spikes hidden beneath the surface of the water.

- 25E3
- Visitor information 538 2332
- If not on a tour, take a picnic
- Can be visited on a whale-watching tour (► 54) or by water taxi from Samaná dock
- Arroya Barril, Samaná

ISLA DE CAYO LEVANTADO

Tour operators usually drop you at Isla de Cayo Levantado (Cayo Levantado Island) after whale-watching in the Bahía de Samaná. This offshore island, coated with tropical forest and boasting a trio of beaches, gets grossly overcrowded, especially at weekends. Its arresting white bay, where pelicans dive bomb into the ocean for fish, is supposedly where a Bacardi drinks commercial was filmed. The main beach, bedecked with dining tables and shacks selling *coco-loco* and poor souvenirs, is often packed with tour groups having buffet lunches.

- 25D4
- San Juan
- Daily
- Choice nearby (£–££)
- Express bus to San Juan from Santo Domingo then *gua-gua*
- Cheap

LAGUNA GRI-GRI

Laguna Gri-Gri (Gri-Gri Lagoon), a popular day trip, usually involves a bus ride to Río San Juan fishing village and then a two-hour boat ride through the mangroves and out onto the ocean. Charter your own boat if you wish. Look out for strange rock formations, caves of stalactites, stalagmites and swallow birds. Remember to take insect spray and a towel because there's a refreshing swimming spot.

MUSEO DE AMBAR DOMINICANO ✪✪✪

The Museo de Ambar Dominicano (Dominican Amber Museum) in Puerto Plata is one of the best places to see amber. Occupying a brilliant-white, 19th-century building, that was a hotel then a school, the museum is marked by its own version of the Jurassic Park movie logo. The second floor of the museum boasts a scorpion, a praying mantis, petals and leaves fossilised in chunks of amber. The priceless trapped lizard has been dated at 50 million years old. The museum's English-speaking guide whisks you round the artefacts, and demonstrates how to distinguish fake, plastic 'amber' jewellery from the real thing by dropping each into water. Larimar is particularly exquisite when set in silver – the museum has a stunning collection.

- 24C4
- Calle Duarte 61, Puerto Plata
- 586 2848/586 3910
- Daily 9–5, closed Sun
- Good choice in Puerto Plata (£–££)
- None
- Cheap
- Gral G Luperón, Puerto Plata

DID YOU KNOW?

Although it gave the colour its name, amber varies with age; as a rule, the darker the amber, the older it is – some fragments are red or black. Just to complicate matters, unique to the Dominican Republic is blue amber; it's expensive too.

PARQUE LUPERÓN ✪✪

The heart of Puerto Plata (➤ 21) is Parque Luperón (Luperón Park), commonly known as Parque Central. Its pretty Glorieta Sicilian pavilion was built in 1872. Nineteenth-century buildings, including the town hall and law courts, surround the park. Sit on a bench and watch the shoeshine boys get to work polishing leather. The pink art deco Catedral de San Felipe is worth a peek inside. From here thread streets of cafés, more gingerbread-style houses, the Museo de Ambar Dominicano (➤ above) boutiques and souvenir shops.

- 24C4
- Puerto Plata
- Good choice nearby (£–££)
- None
- Cheap
- Gral G Luperón, Puerto Plata

The Dominican Republic is famed for its hand-crafted amber jewellery

Amber Coast

Although amber is mined further inland, the coastal strip from east to west is nicknamed the Amber Coast. Driving westwards, expect to meet cattle being driven by boys on horseback and chickens crossing the road. Children straddle donkeys carrying pales of water and vegetables.

From Cabarete head along Carretera 2, through palms and mahogany trees, passing airport signs and big resorts until you reach Sosúa.

Strolling along the shoreline of Sosúa on the Amber Coast

Distance
176km maximum

Time
Full day

Start point
Cabarete
✚ 24C4

End point
Parque Nacional La Isabela or Monte Cristi
✚ 24B4/24A4

Lunch
Numerous in Puerto Plata or Rancho del Sol, Parque Nacional La Isabela (£–££)

To see Sosúa beach, park on the right, just before the village (look out for the black and white Harrison sign) and walk down the stone steps.

Continue on the same road towards Puerto Plata and either explore the town or make your way to Luperón (first following signs to Santiago before sighting the detour to Luperón).

The route is through crops of coffee, avocados, corn and bananas. Sugarcane fields are dotted with royal palms. Notice the average house is a simple *bohío*, similar to the wooden-slatted shacks occupied by the Taino Indians. Despite their primitive appearance, the *bohíos* are well-kept and painted in striking pinks, greens and blues.

From here the way is signposted to Parque Nacional La Isabela (► 19). Once you've explored the park, continue past the church.

In 1992, Mass was said by the Pope here, to commemorate Columbus's discovery.

You can either retrace your journey back to Cabarete or head for a longer stay at Puerto Plata and the Museo de Ambar Dominicano (Dominican Amber Museum, ► 43).

DID YOU KNOW?

The first mass was held in the Dominican Republic on 6 January 1494 by Father Fray Bernando Boil at La Isabela, now the Parque Nacional La Isabela (► 19).

PARQUE NACIONAL LOS HAÏTISES ✪

To the south of the Bahía de Samaná, Parque Nacional Los Haïtises (National Park Los Haïtises) is a microcosm of limestone hillocks covered with tropical humid forest, bamboo, swamp and coral knolls that jut out into the ocean.

Birds thrive here, particularly the elusive Hispaniolan parakeet, herons and American frigates. Other attractions are the Taino caves decorated with drawings and rock carvings. This is a remote, rugged and ungroomed park, so it's best to visit with an organised tour which traverses one of the few trails.

25D3
National parks office
472 4204

DID YOU KNOW?

Spanish is the official language of the Dominican Republic. Around 75 per cent of the population is Roman Catholic. Their ancestry is a mixture of Spanish settlers and African slaves.

PARQUE NACIONAL LA ISABELA (➤ 19, TOP TEN)

PARQUE NACIONAL MONTE CRISTI ✪✪

The Parque Nacional Monte Cristi (National Park Monte Cristi) gives you a feeling of being in the Australian outback, although pure white sands, aqua-blue oceans and mangroves remind you it's the Caribbean. A motor boat takes you across the coastal swamp to a wooden lookout tower to spot manatees. To date it's mainly Dominicans who swim from the beautiful beach and picnic here on Sundays, though it has obvious potential for development as an adventure destination. There are plans to create a surfaced road. For now either take a 4WD along the bumpy access road or book a tour to the Haitian border that includes Parque Nacional La Isabela and Monte Cristi.

24A4
Caño Estero Hondo, Bay of La Isabela
National park office 472 4204
Daily
Take a picnic
Few
Cheap
Use mosquito repellent, and wear a sun hat

The little-known picnic spot of Parque Nacional Monte Cristi

PENÍNSULA DE SAMANÁ (➤ 13, TOP TEN)

PICO ISABEL DE TORRES ✪✪

Named by Columbus after the Queen of Spain, Pico Isabel de Torres is the unmistakable, 800m peak, thickly clad with green vegetation, that towers over Puerto Plata. On its slopes is a scientific reserve while the top has a botanical garden, magnificent views and Cristo Redentor, a statue of Christ. Depending on whether the Caribbean's only electric chairlift, the volatile *teléferico*, is working, you might be able to ride for 13 minutes to the summit. For now you can drive to it (4WD recommended) or hike, or mountain-bike downwards from the peak.

- 24C4
- Chairlift closed Wed
- 970 0501
- Tours with Iguana Mama 571 0908

Opposite: *when Columbus saw the mountain of the north, he named it Pico Isabela de Torres after his Spanish Queen*

PLAYA DORADA ✪

Playa Dorada is the biggest resort complex in the Caribbean, sprawling over 100 hectares and edged by a 3km, caramel-coloured curve of sand. Guests at its 14 all-inclusive hotels are identified by different-coloured plastic bracelets. Despite its 4,500-plus rooms, between February and March you'd be hard-pressed to find a bed – booking ahead is highly recommended. The 18-hole Robert Trent Jones golf course (which boasts 10 tees overlooking the Atlantic Ocean) and a shopping plaza within the complex supplement each hotel's own restaurants, nightclubs and casinos. Non-residents can sometimes buy a day pass. Walk the beach, ride the banana boat, rest under a palm umbrella or snorkel off the stone jetties. Towards the western stretch of beach, low tide exposes a patchwork of seaweed-strewn rock pools where children gather to watch the fish.

- 24C4
- Puerto Plata
- 320 3988 (Passes available depending on season)
- Numerous (£–££)
- Good
- Gral G Luperón, Puerto Plata

Below: *guests practise their swings at the Robert Trent Golf Course at the resort of Playa Dorada*

PLAYA GRANDE ✪

A kilometre long with high cliffs and shaded by palm trees, Playa Grande is one of the finest beaches in the country. An upmarket resort, popular with golfers playing at the reputable Robert Trent Jones course.

- 25D4
- Along the coast (£–££)

Food & Drink

Sticking to the all-inclusive buffet just because you've paid for it doesn't mean you can't be adventurous one day and eat out. Dominican food is nothing if not varied, handed down from the Spanish colonisers, native Indians and African slaves.

Good snacks
Batatas – baked sweet potatoes, delicious cold and slightly charred
pastelitos – pasties filled with meat, raisins and egg, or just cheese
empanadas – similar pasties made with *yuca* (cassava) flour
fritos maduros – fried plantains
guarapo – sugarcane juice
pollo frito – fried chicken
chicharones – pork crackling

In the capital, Santo Domingo, Japanese sushi bars rub shoulders with French cuisine and clay-oven baked pizzas. What you get is a basic melting pot with cassava, sweet potato, bean, fish, spices, carrots, artichokes and bananas to name a few, jazzed up with fashionable trends.

Meals

Breakfast can be muffins, waffles and *Café Santo Domingo* at the patisseries of Cabarete, or eggs and *mangú* (mashed plantains and onions) served at a beach bar. The main meal is lunch, maybe *la bandera* – a mix of rice with red beans and meats – followed by a blissful siesta. The national dish is *sancocho*, a stew made with pork, beef, chicken or goat and vegetables, with a round of cassava bread. (In the Dominican Alps you can see cassava bread being made by hand in the Taino way.)

Coconuts, sugarcane, oranges and onions on a mountain road

Plantains
Plantains belong to the banana family. They are green and Dominicans eat them fried, sometimes in batter. The southwest is noted for the size of its plantains and the local men brag about them.

Left: *plantains grow big on the hot plains*
Below: *a platter of freshly caught and grilled seafood is served alfresco*

Seafood
Dominican seafood is absolutely superb, ranging from grilled shrimps, langoustine and lobster to sea bass and kingfish. *Pescado con coco* is fish cooked in a delicious coconut and cream sauce. The meat of the conch shell (*lambi*), usually marinated and served with salad, is thought to be an aphrodisiac.

Drinks
An ideal cure for a hangover is *guarapo*, thick sugarcane juice. To need it in the first place, try '151 Rum' – 75 per cent proof! *Ron* (rum) is, of course, the national drink. It comes in light, golden or dark and aged varieties. The most popular brands are Brugal, Bermudez and Barceló. Presidente beer is advertised everywhere and is best drunk ice cold from the bottle. Cocktails are plenty. Cuba Libre is rum and coke, a coco-loco is coconut milk and rum actually served in the coconut, and a Banana Mama is a non-alcoholic cocktail – banana with fresh fruits and grenadine. Other non-alcoholic drinks popular with Dominicans are orange juice (which they sweeten heavily with sugar) and fruit punch. Although known brands of soft drinks are sold, an instant refresher is a *tierno*, a soft coconut bought by the roadside. After drinking its juice through a straw, find a spoon and devour the succulent flesh.

Fruit and Desserts
Within the country's ample fruit bowl are coconuts, guavas, oranges, mangoes, passion fruit and grapefruit and, grown in the Cordillera Central, apples and strawberries. Desserts are called *dulces* and can be excruciatingly sweet. Try *flan de piña* (pineapple custard) or *arroz con leche* (rice pudding).

DID YOU KNOW?
The Dominican Republic is world famous for premium-quality cigars. The most expensive is Arturo Fuente at around US$250 for a box of 25. Other top brands include Fuente Opus X and Partagas Limited Reserve Royale. Fine cigars, like fine wines, come in a flavour spectrum from mild, fruity and chocolatey to strong and spicy.

Around Puerto Plata

Distance
Around 2km

Time
Half a day

Start/end point
Parque Luperón
24C4

Lunch
Numerous in town (£–££)

Although some of Puerto Plata's 100,000 inhabitants still work in the sugarcane trade and agriculture, many more now work in tourism at resorts along the north coast and supporting services.

At the start point, Parque Luperón (➤ 43), you can bargain with a guide who will show you the sights. Some are very knowledgeable on the history and this is their only form of work. Prices can be reasonable. Alternatively do-it-yourself around this compact place. Before you start, admire the Glorieta Sicilian pavilion and visit the Catedral de San Felipe.

Cross over to the white church on the corner with Calle Beller. If it's Sunday morning, you might hear Mass and hymn singing. Head back towards the cathedral and turn right down Calle Duarte.

Notice the Victorian gingerbread decoration on the houses and ornate verandas. Notice too, how chunks of this architecture have been knocked down to make way for something modern and concrete.The Museo de Ambar Dominicano (Dominican Amber Museum) (➤ 43) is easy to detect. Spot the red and black *Jurassic Park* logos on a pure white building.

Retrace your steps back towards the cathedral and square, but turn right and continue all the way up Separación until the street meets with Av. Gregorio Luperón, the malecón by the oceanfront. Enjoy the views before turning left towards the Fuerte de San Felipe (➤ 42).

Around the base of the fort walls are hawkers selling souvenirs.

From here head back to the square along José del Carmen Ariza for some serious souvenir shopping down the main thoroughfares of Calle Beller and Calle Duarte.

Top: *pastel-coloured chalets at the Puerto Plata Village resort*
Above: *the Amber Museum displays fossils and jewellery*
Opposite: *Parque Luperón in Puerto Plata*

SANTIAGO DE LOS CABALLEROS

- 24C4
- Good choice of cafés and restaurants (£–££)
- Express bus from Santo Domingo and Puerto Plata
- Few
- Cheap
- English-speaking guides offer tours
- Cibao, Santiago

At the heart of the country's tobacco industry and set within the fertile Valle Cibao (Cibao Valley) is Santiago de los Caballeros, the country's second largest city. Known simply as Santiago, the place buzzes day and night – what *merengue* is not played on street corners is blasted from passing cars that are patched and home-painted.

Present-day Santiago sprawls on the banks of the Río Yaque del Norte. (The city founded by Bartolomé Columbus in 1495 at another site was largely destroyed by the 1562 earthquake.) Aside from the Monumento a los Héroes de la Restauración de la República (Heroes Monument, ➤ 18), Santiago has a handful of attractions. Although not as pretty as Puerto Plata's main square, Parque Duarte (Duarte Park) has the ubiquitous shoeshine boys and *merengue* cassette music sellers. The Museo del Tabaco (Tobacco Museum) traces the history of the uses of tobacco from the 16th century. Provided you are smartly dressed, you can glimpse inside the grand, members-only Centro de Recreo club, built in 1894. Next door is a Palacio Consistorial gallery, the former town hall, and quite empty apart from whatever temporary exhibitions it is hosting at the time, maybe carnival masks, sculpture or paintings. The 19th-century Catedral Santiago Apòstol, as pink as a birthday cake, has an interior of mahogany, brightly coloured stained glass and gold leaf.

If you just want to shop, Santiago has roughly made, cheap and cheerful clothing, watches, wallets, leather shoes, carnival masks, spinning hoops and fast food. It also has noisy traffic, deeply guttered streets, and overhead intertwined electricity cables which have an annoying habit of getting in the way of your photographs.

Below: *the noisy, lively streets of downtown Santiago*
Inset: *Sociedad Centro de Recreo, an exclusive billiard club in central Santiago*

SOSÚA

Away from the busy main highway, Sosúa consists of leafy lanes of bars, boutiques and restaurants serving Italian, Mexican and – more unusually – much German fayre. In 1940 many Jewish refugees from Nazi Europe settled here. It has been suggested that dictator Trujillo was keen to earn international respect, or that he wanted to 'whiten' his country after years of black Haitian immigration. Anyway, Trujillo set aside a portion of land for the Jewish immigrants to work. The Jews, however, were not farmers but intellectuals and businessmen. Still, they brought their tastes with them and made Sosúa famous for its butter, cheese and sausages. Few Jewish houses remain, though the synagogue can be visited. At one end of town is a mixture of tin roof shacks, at the other the half-moon curve of the popular El Batey bay, a highlight of the north. Reached via a stone flight of stairs, the beach is beyond the network of paintings, cigars, beachwear and even a barber and his chair, ready to cut. Swimming is very safe here – the bay is protected by a coral reef – which is a reason why so many fish are spotted by snorkellers and passengers of glass-bottomed boats. There's a jazz festival every October at venues in both Sosúa and nearby Cabarete, and a sandcastle-building competition is held during February.

- 24C4
- Visitor information 571 3433
- Good choice of cafés and restaurants (£–££)
- *Gua-gua* from Puerto Plata
- Few
- Cheap
- English-speaking guides offer tours
- Gral G Luperón, Puerto Plata

Above: *a ride on a jet ski is just one watersport on offer at Sosúa*

LAS TERRENAS

Although Las Terrenas, originally a fishing village, has been taken over by around a dozen Italian, French and German hotels and a string of restaurants, it is loved by many visitors to the Dominican Republic who shy away from the sprawling all-inclusive resorts. The beaches of El Portillo and quieter Playa Bonita are favourites, offering scuba diving and other watersports. The nearby village of El Limón gives access to the Salto de Caloda, an impressive, high waterfall.

- 25D4
- Good choice of cafés and restaurants (£–££)
- *Gua-gua* or pick-up truck
- Arroya Barril, Samaná

Whale-watching Trip

Tour Operators
Iguana Mama ☎ 571 0908
Whale Samana Victoria Marine ☎ 538 2588

DID YOU KNOW?

You'll not hear them, but male humpback whales sing a song which can be heard by other whales miles away. One theory suggests they are telling the females that they're ready and willing to mate.

With reports of an incredible whale-watching season in 2002 and 2003, the reputation of the Dominican Republic as a whale-watching destination is steadily growing. There's also a much stronger effort afoot to enforce rules for safe and sensitive whale-watching. Boats patrol almost every day around the Bahía de Samaná to make sure operators are respecting these laws. Beware the ultra-cheap whale-watching trips which skimp on safety and space in the boat. Your best bet is to pay a little extra and book a bigger boat with an operator who is sympathetic to the whales and has a canopy to keep off the sun.

From Puerto Plata, for instance, the coach tour passes Sosúa and Cabarete on Carretera 5. The landscape stretches into the distance over rice paddies, coconut and coffee plantations. Villages hang freshly killed pigs out for sale. (Don't look because someone might be sawing through a thigh.)

Right: *wildlife watchers wait patiently as a humpback whale breaks the surface of the waters of the Bahìa de Samaná*

Inset: *a humpback whale waves its giant flipper before slipping back into the ocean*

A stop for buffet breakfast is made at San Juan before heading through Nagua to the docks at Samaná, where you'll board a boat or catamaran for roughly 60–90 minutes of whale-watching in the Bahía de Samaná.

After hopefully a good sighting, you'll be ferried to Isla de Cayo Levantado (➤ 42) for a buffet lunch and live music. The afternoon is then yours to spend sunbathing, snorkelling or strolling across to 'Bacardi beach'. At the end of the day, a boat takes you back across the bay to meet the coach. The journey home might involve a couple of photo stops of the Cibao Valley and a chance to buy rum.

Above: *an enormous show of strength as the humpback whale breaches spectacularly into the air*

Legend says the Basílica de Nuestra Señora de la Altagracia in Higüey is where the Virgin Mary appeared in 1691 and many times since

Southeast

Heading east from Santo Domingo on the Las Américas Highway the landscape pales to dry, flat savannahs. No coffee, tobacco or cocoa grows here, only scrub and sugarcane. At a railway crossing with flashing red lights you may be delayed for a good 10 minutes by a long train, laden with sugarcane stalks, bound for the sugar mill at La Romana. Inland you could make your own pilgrimage to the famous basilica at Higüey.

By the roadside you might see erected branches from which dangle freshly caught river crabs for sale. The region's exquisite beaches offer scores of opportunities for serious relaxation. At the far southeastern tip of the country is beautiful Parque Nacional del Este and the popular Isla Saona. You can travel back in time to the cliff-top village of Altos de Chavón (actually 20th-century but designed to look medieval) or go snorkelling on the coral reefs of Parque Nacional Submarino La Caleta.

What to See in the Southeast

ALTOS DE CHAVÓN (► 12, TOP TEN)

BASÍLICA DE NUESTRA SEÑORA DE LA ALTAGRACIA ✪✪

- 25F2
- Higüey
- Visitor information 554 2672
- Daily
- Few cafés in Higüey (£–££)
- Bus from Santo Domingo
- Good
- Cheap
- Punta Cana, Higüey

Higüey itself is a busy town with little to offer the tourist at first glance. It is, however, the country's most important religious site. Said to be built on the site where the Virgin Mary appeared in 1691, the Basílica de Nuestra Señora de la Altagracia is an extraordinary vision. The French architects André Jacques Dunoyer de Segonzac and Pierre Dupré have shaped its spire into a pair of hands praying. Started in 1952, the cathedral is made from solid concrete in such a way as to withstand a hurricane. Many children beg outside the basilica or sell you candles. Pilgrimages occur on 21 January and 16 August. Pilgrims enter the shrine to La Altagracia (the Virgin of the Highest Grace), framed by mahogany carved into the branches of an orange tree, and touch a glass case displaying a 16th-century painting of the Virgin and a gold crown given as a gift by a former Pope.

BÁVARO ✪✪

Bávaro, on the Costa del Coco (Coconut Coast), is paradise: blue skies, a blue sea and uninterrupted white sands sloping to calm, reef-protected waters. Some of the country's most exclusive resorts lie behind its palm-fringed beach. Holidaymakers go sea fishing for marlin, while others merely tuck into freshly caught lobsters and langoustines grilled out in the open at restaurants scattered across the sands. Musical trios strum guitars and play *merengue* or sing romantic ballads. In short, it's the stuff of dream holidays and honeymoons.

- 25F3
- Costa del Coco
- Good choice (£–££)
- Bus to Higüey, then *gua-gua*
- Punta Aguila, Romana

BAYAHIBE ✪✪

Bayahibe is another idyllic haunt and absolutely gorgeous, a gateway to Parque Nacional del Este (➤ 59). A colourful and hectic fishing village, Bayahibe is engulfed by pale-honey sands shaped as small coves, rolling down to azure lapping waters. Waiting speedboats, catamarans and wooden craft ferry scores of people, towels tucked under their arms, out to Isla Saona (➤ 16, 60). If you haven't already organised a tour, it can prove expensive. Best to share a fishing boat called a *lancha* that works like a taxi – the more passengers, the cheaper the fare. Alternatively, there's an excellent diving centre and cold beer at the nearby cafés.

- 25E2
- Cafés nearby (£)

Splendid Bayahibe beach is the embarkation point for day trips to Isla Saona

- 25E2
- Hotel La Romana
- 523 3333
- Mixed choice (££–£££)
- Good
- Punta Aguila, Romana

CASA DE CAMPO

The resort of Casa de Campo at La Romana is today as big as a town, and has been dubbed 'the Caribbean's most complete resort' now with a marina and yacht club and Portofino, a shopping and dining area. La Romana had been the country's primary sugar production centre, but sugar production was taken over by industrial free trade zones, tobacco and the then new 'industry' of tourism. The mega-rich sugar plantation owners anticipated these changes and diversified by building or buying hotels and resorts. In the 1960s the US company, Gulf & Western, bought the sugar mill and invested heavily in La Romana. To entertain their visitors and top executives they transformed the Hotel La Romana into today's exclusive resort (although it's no longer owned by Gulf & Western). Casa de Campo suffered badly during Hurricane Georges in 1998 and has since been spectacularly rebuilt to the tune of US$24 million. It boasts championship-rated 18-hole golf courses, designed by Pete Dye, polo, clay pigeon shooting and all kinds of watersports.

DID YOU KNOW?

Champion player and Indian prince, Maharajah Jabar Singh introduced polo to the Dominican Republic in 1954 when he was invited to teach Trujillo's sons. In 1970, Singh began developing polo at Casa de Campo, where it has flourished ever since. Matches are played regularly from November to mid-May.

ISLA SAONA (SAONA ISLAND) **(➤ 16, TOP TEN; 60)**

Casa de Campo, the biggest resort in the country, knows how to entertain the kids

Taino Indian graves uncovered at Parque Nacional Submarino La Caleta

PARQUE NACIONAL DEL ESTE ✪✪✪

The fabulous Parque Nacional del Este (National Park of the East) is a ribbon of jade green sandwiched between a blue sky and a blue-green ocean. Here are breathtaking beauty, wildlife and solitude – its only human inhabitants live on Isla Saona (➤ 16, 60) but look out for iguanas, and, offshore, dolphins and turtles. The park's limestone terraces are clothed with a mixture of subtropical humid, dry and deciduous forests. Its many limestone caves – José Maria Cave especially – are decorated with pre-Columbian petroglyphs and pictographs. Best access is by boat, perhaps as part of a day trip to Isla Saona. This can be organised in your resort or in Bayahibe (➤ 57).

- 25F2
- National parks office 472 4204
- Daily
- None
- Boat trips arranged through operators

PARQUE NACIONAL SUBMARINO LA CALETA ✪

From Santo Domingo the coastal road runs through groves of almond trees and palms. Roadside vendors sell carved pieces of calcium from the caves, etched bookends and other Taino-style souvenirs. You'll reach Parque Nacional Submarino La Caleta (Submarino La Caleta National Park), the smallest in the country. Between coral cliffs, its sandy cove has upturned fishing boats. You can swim and snorkel from here in shallow water, around a number of coral reefs sporting tropical fish and octopuses. Divers and underwater photographers especially find the sunken 20th-century wreck, the *Hickory*, of interest. Sadly, on land the park is badly kept, but the untidy one-storey building near the entrance is actually a museum sheltering a remarkable Indian cemetery, found in 1972 and excavated. The Indians buried their dead near the sea, in easily dug sand. The haunting collection of skeletons, buried in the foetal position to await reincarnation, is at times grotesque, for when a chief died it was customary to bury his wife, alive, with him.

- 25D2
- National parks office 472 4204
- Daily
- *Gua-gua* from Santo Domingo
- None
- Cheap

Isla Saona (Saona Island)

Distance
30 km

Time
Full day

Start/end point
Altos de Chavón or Bayahibe
25E2
Book through your resort or hire a boat from Bayahibe

Lunch
Usually provided by the tour and taken on the island. Otherwise buy provisions at the French bakery at Altos de Chavón or take a picnic. Don't forget drinking water, sunscreen and a camera, and hiking boots if going to the caves.

Opposite: *palms cast a shadow onto the sands of Isla Saona*
Below: *sightseeing boats on the Río Chavón prepare for a day's paddle upstream*

Either arrange a tour through your hotel or resort, or arrive at Bayahibe beach and book a transfer. More sightseeing can be had if you hire a fishing boat from the steps of Altos de Chavón (➤ 12).

The Mediterranean village of Altos de Chavón perches on the cliff tops as you chug through a corridor of palms, passing other people in boats, fishing. Boca de Chavón fishing village approaches as you turn left at the river mouth, into the expanse of Caribbean Sea. Heading east along this coastline you can see the extent of the all-inclusives. Guests perform aerobics on the beach, or paddle in kayaks, or try desperately to stay on windsurfers.

Suddenly the resorts thin out and disappear as you enter Parque Nacional del Este (➤ 59). Only forests, palm trees and sand line the shore. A boy riding his horse bareback might appear.

The water here is calm and clear. Part of the way your boat stops at a natural swimming pool where starfish rest on the seabed a few metres below. If you wish, you can take a dip or enjoy a drink from the boat's onboard icebox.

The boat continues through a lagoon lined with black and red mangroves between the mainland and Isla Saona. Finally arriving at the island, you head first to look at paintings and souvenirs in the fishing village. A two-minute journey then whisks you to the main beach, Punta Catuano, to relax for some hours until the boat returns the same way. See also ➤ 16.

Legacy of the Tainos

National Parks Office
☎ 472 4204
Check in advance that the sites are open.

By the early 1500s the Taino population of the island of Hispaniola, estimated at 1 million when Columbus arrived in 1492, had been reduced to around 500. Disease, forced slavery and labour, massacre and even suicide were responsible for obliterating an indigenous people who could have contributed much to the New World.

Today, the legacy of the Tainos lives on in at least 40 known sites of petroglyphs and cave art, many of which have been archaeologically investigated. Caves held special significance, often used for sacred ceremonies and rituals, and guarded by fearsome gods. A few are open to tourists and some have guided tours, which can be booked through your resort. Here are the most popular sites, but always check well in advance to make sure they are open.

Cueva de las Maravillas in Boca de Soco, is on the San Pedro de Macoris road to La Roma. Known locally as the 'cave of wonders', two caves, with drawings, stalactites and stalagmites, were probably used for Taino rituals.

The Anthropological Reserve of Cuevas de Borbón in San Cristóbal (► 67) was extended in 1996 to protect the **Cueva de Pommiers** or **El Pomier** caves threatened by limestone quarrying. One of the most extensive examples of prehistoric art yet discovered in the Caribbean, the caves contain works by Igneri and Carib Indians as well as the Taino. More than 4,000 wall paintings and 5,000 rock drawings depict birds crouching with wings folded and people catching birds in their hands.

Parque Nacional del Este (► 59) is famous for some of the most fascinating Taino sites ever discovered, including the oldest drawings which archaeologists believe could be up to 2,000 years old. Indiana University has carried out extensive research here, including investigations of the Jose Maria Cave and also Manatial de le Aleta, a deep limestone grotto filled with crystal clear water. See drawings and carvings of mating birds, fish, lizards and sketches in charcoal.

A useful introduction to the Taino Indians is at the Museo del Hombre Dominicano (Museum of Dominican Man) in Santo Domingo (► 35). You can also view a typical Taino burial ground at Parque Nacional Submarino La Caleta (► 59).

Taino exhibit in the Museo del Hombre Dominicano

PLAYA BOCA CHICA (➤ 20, TOP TEN)

PUNTA CANA ✪✪

Punta Cana is a sight to behold. Singer Juglio Iglesias and Dominican-born fashion designer Oscar de la Renta have properties here and are co-developers of the Punta Cana Resort, a luxurious retreat with a flower-shaped pool yards from a talcum-powder white beach with swaying palms. The orange-red sunsets are a picture. Punta Cana's own, remarkable international airport will even accommodate Boeing 747s. Built from the Punta Cana tree and topped with a thatched roof, the tropical airport building has check-in desks of purple, red and blue, and an equally colourful VIP lounge complete with internet stations.

25F2
Buses from Higüey
Punta Cana, Higüey

SAN PEDRO DE MACORÍS ✪✪

San Pedro de Macorís is a big, busy, and – thanks to the American occupation – a baseball-crazy town. It lies on the Río Higuamo, where the Americans landed in seaplanes. Good sugarcane yields in the early 20th century made the town rich, reflected in its grand Victorian architecture. Only a few beauties exist, including the English Gothic, brilliant-white Iglesia San Pedro. A more contemporary building, which takes pride of place in the town, is a green-topped baseball stadium. The town's massive industrial free-trade zone makes clothing and other goods. San Pedro de Macorís is home to some of the best baseball players in the world, including Sammy Sosa (➤ 10) who was born here. They say chewing the sweet fibres off bark-like sticks of sugarcane made the budding young players strong. This is also the base for exploring Cueva de las Maravillas, a cave of rock paintings from the Tainos period. The opening of the cave is controversial, especially since the installation of lights and elevators.

25E2
Few cafés in town (£–££)
Gua-gua from Santo Domingo

Below: *a banana seller sets up his barrow in the streets of San Pedro de Macorís*

DID YOU KNOW?

The shopping centre at 3030 Plaza was so-called after baseball star Sammy Sosa hit 30 home runs and stole 30 bases. Within the centre is a children's clinic founded by the player, and a comically small statue dedicated to him; the plaque at his feet reads '*Fuente del Limpiabotus*' (fountain of the shoe cleaner).

Southwest

Heading from Santo Domingo towards the Haitian border, the landscape has yet to be swallowed by all-inclusives, though tourism is developing gradually. Dry deserts one minute, waterfalls cascading down tropical peaks the next, the southwest is like nowhere else in the Dominican Republic. Bends in the recently surfaced Carretera Sánchez highway reveal ragged low cliffs and white surf through the palms. Visitors come for the nature, uncrowded beaches, smelly but therapeutic sulphur springs and ecologically fascinating national parks. Driving west out of Azua de Compostela you'll see the scrub and cacti of the Sierra de Martín Garcia – it could be the Spanish highlands, but then the Caribbean Sea comes into view and all is tropical and green again.

What to See in the Southwest

AZUA DE COMPOSTELA ✪

24C2
Few in town (£)
Express bus from Santo Domingo

A convenient stopping point as you head further west, Azua de Compostela has a turbulent history. Founded in 1504 by Diego Velâsquez, who accompanied Christopher Columbus on his second voyage to Hispaniola, the town has seen many battles between Dominicans and Haitians (as well as earthquakes). The town park was created to honour those who fought for the area's independence in 1844.

BANÍ ✪✪

24C2
Few in town (£)
Gua-gua from Santo Domingo

Baní lies off the main southwest route, the Carretera Sánchez. It's known for its small, sweet, red mangoes, though the area's varied agricultural produce also includes tomatoes, plantains, cashew nuts and red onions. Baní was the birthplace of General Máximo Gómez, 'the liberator of Cuba', who helped lead the revolution against the Spaniards and which resulted in Cuba's independence. Casa de Máximo Gómez is a museum devoted to the general. Strolling around Parque Duarte is very pleasant, and the salt pans of La Salinas, set among sand dunes, are around 45 minutes' drive away.

Right: *trailing through Isla Cabritos in search of iguanas and crocodiles*
Inset: *an iguana shelters beneath the cacti on Isla Cabritos*

BARAHONA ✪✪

Barahona is a seaside town on the Península Pedernales, noted for its scientific reserves and its wildlife. Founded in 1802 by a Haitian and exploited for sugarcane by dictator Trujillo, Barahona still thrives on sugar – the chimneys spouting from the quivering plantations belong to the mills. Workers often set fire to parts of the fields so the stalks are easier to cut. The scene is pretty scary and the heat intense.

24B2
Tourist information 524 3650
Express bus from Santo Domingo
María Montez, Barahona

ISLA CABRITOS ✪✪✪

Isla Cabritos (Goat Island) takes its name from the goats that once grazed there. The 12km-long island is within the small Parque Nacional Isla Cabritos. Combined with salty Lago Enriquillo and its American crocodiles (► 17, 68), it makes for a fantastic day out. Used as a refuge and supply centre for Indian chief Enriquillo, the island was ceded to a French family during the years of Haitian occupation. It was declared a national park in 1974. A round of dry, parched desert, the island is home to two species of iguana, the *ricordi* and the *rhinoceros*, which are unfortunately too friendly and run up to you expecting food. More than 100 types of plant have been recorded and 10 varieties of cactus which produce colourful flowers and trick you into thinking this is America's Wild West. Remember to wear strong, covered footwear as scorpions scuttle in the sand.

24A2
Parque Nacional Isla Cabritos
National parks office 472 4204
Daily
None
Moderate
Permit required, must be accompanied by a guide

PARQUE NACIONAL JARAGUA ✪✪

- 24A1
- Barahona Peninsula
- National parks office 472 4204
- Daily
- None
- Cheap
- Best visited on organised tour

Parque Nacional Jaragua (Jaragua National Park), at the southernmost tip of the country, is the largest protected area on the island. This is the place of the 4WD, popular with birdwatchers, but remote. Principally dry forest, with two offshore islands, the park is hot and arid with beaches and a lagoon with a large flamingo colony. Among its birdlife 60 per cent of the country's species are reportedly represented, along with iguanas, and the four marine turtles common here: hawksbill, leatherback, loggerhead and green. Undoubtedly there are yet more caves from the Taino period showing pictographs and petroglyphs.

The green turtle can be seen in its natural habitat in the Parque Nacional Jaragua

PARQUE NACIONAL SIERRA DE BAORUCO ✪✪

- 24A2
- National parks office 472 4204
- Daily 8–5
- Tour operator or *gua-gua* from Barahona
- None
- Cheap

The aridity and isolation of Parque Nacional Sierra de Baoruco (Sierra de Baoruco National Park) may deter many holidaymakers, but those who make the effort are treated to mountains as high as 2,367m, a plethora of birds and over 50 per cent of all the country's native orchid species. In these mountains the Taino Indian chief, Enriquillo, fought for his tribe's freedom against the Spaniards in the 1500s, declaring a small republic on top of the sierra.

PLAYA SAN RAFAEL ✪✪✪

- 24B2
- *Gua-gua* from Barahona

Dominicans from the capital often spend their leisure time at Playa San Rafael, chilling Presidente beer in the cool sulphur springs, before taking a dip in either the waterfall-fed lagoon or the sea. If you're hungry, don't worry because usually there's someone cooking fresh fish in the open air.

RESERVA ANTROPOLÓGICA CUEVAS DE EL POMIER ✪✪✪

The world's principal Taino archaeological location, Reserva Antropológica Cuevas de El Pomier consists of 54 caves decorated with thousands of pictographs (wall drawings) and petroglyphs (rock carvings), as well as stalactites and stalagmites. Located 7km from San Cristóbal, near a limestone quarry, they were discovered in 1851 by Sir Robert Schonburgk, a British consul for the Dominican Republic. About a dozen caves are open for viewing. Cave Number One alone is blessed with 590 pictographs. Expect to also see aboriginal graves, ceramic and indigenous oddments (and a lot of bats).

- 24C2
- Borbón Section, near San Cristóbal
- National parks office 472 4204
- Daily
- None
- Cheap

Above: *a good harvest of plantains winds its way through the streets of San Cristóbal*

SAN CRISTÓBAL ✪

San Cristóbal was the birthplace, in 1891, of dictator Rafael Leonidas Trujillo, who ruled the country ruthlessly from 1930 until his assassination in 1961. During his lifetime Trujillo transformed San Cristóbal into another of his showpieces. He lived in a country home called Casa de Caobas (the Mahogany House). Elsewhere, a dirt track winds uphill to Castillo de Cerro (the Mountain Castle) which he built but never inhabited after hearing someone remark on how hideous it looked. This ugly, dilapidated pale-yellow structure, stamped with white stars, is now in the hands of the army and is not open to the public. It is, however, used by the neighbourhood as a shelter during hurricanes.

Driving round the town takes you past jails so close to the road that you can see the inmates staring back at you. The neo-classical church, Parroquia de Nuestra Señora de Consolación, supposedly contained Trujillo's body in the family vault. Although he lay in state here, it's thought his corpse was transferred to France.

- 24C2
- Casa Las Caobas 528 3553
- Bus from Santo Domingo
- None

DID YOU KNOW?

The first Constitution of the Dominican Republic was signed in San Cristóbal on November 6, 1844, following independence from Haiti.

Lago Enriquillo and the Haitian Border

This drive visits Lago Enriquillo (Lake Enriquillo) (► 17) and Parque Nacional Isla Cabritos (Isla Cabritos National Park) (► 65). Start early because morning is the best time to see the American crocodiles.

Distance
290km

Time
Full day

Start/end point
Santo Domingo
25D2
Bring sunhat, sunblock, mosquito repellent, drinking water and wear covered walking shoes.

Lunch
Good choice on the road, plus cashew nuts and other local snacks.

Head west along Carretera 2, through the towns of San Cristóbal (► 67), Baní (► 64) and Azua de Compostela (► 64). The road changes to Carretera 44, and just before Barahona there's a right turn on to Carretera 48. At Neiba is the lake's loop road, paved and easy to follow; go either left or right.

If you take the right side of the lake, look out for Los Carritas, sad and happy faces in the rock above the road on the right hand side. Many people believe they date back to the Taino period. At the lake a small boat ferries you across to Isla Cabritos, followed by a half-hour walk to see the crocodiles, and probably a flock of pink flamingos launching into the sky. (If you don't wish to visit the island, there are plenty of iguanas on the shoreline and the odd splash from a crocodile.) Later, cool off at the park's swimming pool and have an ice-cold drink from the bar.

Continue to La Descubierto.

Here you can have another swim in the sulphur pool, reached through a forest of tall, red mango trees.

As the border with Haiti approaches the security controls increase and the radio automatically switches to stations playing Creole music. Finally, the border town of Jimaní comes into view.

Here you can browse round a market of tinned pilchards, cooking oil, known brands of whisky, brandy and Babincourt rum (famous in Haiti).

Circle the other side of the lake and, at Neiba, retrace your route back to Santo Domingo.

Above: *Isla Cabritos is the best place to watch American crocodiles basking in the sun*
Opposite: *a refreshing dip in the sulphur pool at La Descubierto*

Cordillera Central

Away from the hotspots on the coast, the mountains of the Cordillera Central (➤ 14–15) are cool, prone to showers and incredibly beautiful. Although some parts of the mountain range are rugged, inhospitable and eroded by deforestation, there are gems, including lush green valleys sprouting potatoes, flowers and strawberries, and where locals use mules as the mode of transport.

Here is where you head if you take a safari from your resort, or if you are adventurous enough to climb Pico Duarte, the Caribbean's highest peak. You can reach the mountains within two to four hours' drive and even stay overnight at one of the many Alpine-style hotels in Jarabacoa (➤ 71). Poking up between pine treetops are wealthy Dominican's grand hilltop mansions and retreats.

DID YOU KNOW?

Mañana in Spanish means tomorrow and is a local laid-back approach to life and decisions. Dominicans hate to displease and so will often say something will be done *mañana*, rather than say never.

What to See in Cordillera Central

CONSTANZA ✪✪

24C3
La Vega

Ringed by glorious mountains, the town of Constanza stands at an altitude of about 1,300m. It's a pretty, quiet place which makes an excellent base for walks. Many farms here belong to Japanese families brought in by Trujillo in the 1950s specifically to cultivate vegetables and fruit. Constanza is noted for its abundance of flowers, garlic and strawberries, growing in a picturesque valley.

Cyclists race through the village of Jarabacoa in celebration of the country's independence

The cool waters and lush vegetation of Jarabacoa make it popular destination with tourists

JARABACOA ✪✪

Set in a sheltered mountain valley, Jarabacoa is best known for its waterfalls. Nowadays it's becoming more popular as a summer hilltop resort and adventure walks tourism centre. Activities on offer include walks through the mountains and foothills, jeep safaris (► 72), ballooning, cycling and horse riding, for example. You can swim in the refreshing pool, La Confluencia, in the Río Jimenoa (but be careful of the currents). Plus, of course, you can raft or just photograph Yaque del Norte, the longest and most important river, which descends as a series of waterfalls. Some 14 rivers have their source in the Cordillera Central. Many people visit Jarabacoa purely to see the waterfalls. By far the greatest is the 40m El Salto de Jimenoa, which involves negotiating a steep trail and bridges to its edge. Another popular cascade is the shorter Salto de Baiguate which can be reached by foot or on horseback. Another deviation is the nearby Ramrez Factory, where selection of the finest coffee beans for toasting is done by hand. There's a 45-minute tour, and you're welcome to taste the coffee.

24C3
La Vega
Rancho Restaurant, Jarabacoa (££) 574 6890/2618

Ramrez Factory
Mon–Sat 8–6

PARQUE NACIONAL ARMANDO BERMÚDEZ & PARQUE NACIONAL JOSÉ DEL CARMEN RAMÍREZ ✪✪✪

Since Columbus' arrival on the island of Hispaniola, it is estimated that two-thirds of the virgin forest in the Dominican Republic has been wiped out. Today Parque Nacional Armando Bermúdez (Armando Bermúdez National Park) and Parque Nacional José del Carmen Ramírez (José del Carmen Ramírez National Park) are the only remaining areas of extensive forests in these mountains. Their role of protection has helped towards retaining what's left and there's even a programme of reforestation underway. In September 1998 Hurricane Georges destroyed river bridges and felled many pines. The bridges have since been rebuilt and the timber is being utilised. Naturally, the wildlife here abounds. Look out for the Hispaniolan parrot, palm chats, doves and warblers. And, in more remote areas, wild boars forage – it's all a far cry from the buffet queues of the all-inclusives.

24B3
National parks office 472 4204
None
Cheap
Permits required, tours and adventure travel (► 84–85)

Jeep Safari

Time
2 hours–half a day

Start/end point
Rancho Baiguate, Jarabacoa
24C3

Lunch
Rancho Baiguate (included in price of tour)
574 6890

This tour takes you to the foothills of the Dominican Alps, through the Jarabacoa Valley to the Salto de Jimenoa waterfall. Go as part of a tour from your resort or book direct through Maxim Aventura, Rancho Baiguate (► 85).

Arrive at Rancho Baiguate for a buffet lunch of typical Dominican food with organic local vegetables and freshly made cassava bread.

You could choose to ride a mule for an hour to the waterfall; otherwise jump into a safari jeep and hang on to the rails as it winds for 15 minutes along country lanes, passing flower nurseries, coffee plantations, and vegetable crops.

Holidaymakers prepare for a day's fun safari in the Cordillera Central

Note the electric lamps suspended above the flowers: when the sun goes down, the light helps keep the flowers growing straight. The tour introduces you to how locals here earn a living by making cassava bread in the traditional way, handed down by the Taino Indians.

You halt at the Río Jimenoa and follow a footpath upstream.

The disused power station on the opposite bank once provided electricity for Jarabacoa but was ravaged by Hurricane Georges in 1998. The river swelled to 10m within hours and destroyed the turbines. It also pulled down tree trunks and huge boulders from the mountains. The boulders toppled to where they now rest, a visible reminder of nature's strength.

The trail leads across suspension bridges, safe yet wobbly.

There's a pool with a small sandy beach where you can take a dip. Before the hurricane it was possible to swim in the pool fed by the waterfall but now the torrent is too fierce. You might see plucky adventurers canyoning down the steep cliffs.

Where To...

Eat and Drink 74–76
Stay 77–79
Shop 80–81
Be Entertained 82–86

Above: *there's so much to do at Puerto Plata Village resort*
Right: *a pair of parrots*

Santo Domingo & Around the Country

Prices
Prices are approximate, based on a three-course meal for one without drinks or service.
£ = under RD$200
££ = RD$200–400
£££ = over RD$400

Taxes and Tipping
A 12 per cent Industrial Goods and Services (ITBIS) tax and a 10 per cent service charge are added to the bill. If you've really enjoyed the food and service, it's customary to add another 10 per cent as a tip.

Santo Domingo

Restaurante Atarazana (££)
Occupying former warehouses a stone's throw from Museo Alcázar de Colón and known for its fish and shrimp dishes.
La Atarazana 5, Zona Colonial 689 2900 Daily, lunch and dinner

Café Bachata Rosa (££)
A virtual museum to the internationally famous Dominican Republic singer, Juan Luis Guerra. Tables resemble the pictures on his CD covers, there are pictures of him and one of his gold discs. Stylish menu with typical Dominican favourites.
La Atarazana, Zona Colonial 688 0969 Nightly until late

Ristorante La Briciola (£££)
Romantic restaurant, half courtyard, half terrace. Excellent Italian food and wine, candlelit tables indoors or within courtyard. There's regular live music from vocalist and pianist.
Arzobispo Meriño, Zona Colonial 688 5055 Daily, lunch–late

Chez Moi (£–££)
Along busy El Conde street, serving chilled pineapple juice, pastas, salads, meat, fish, steaks, wines.
El Conde, Zona Colonial Daily, lunch and evening

Restaurant Conde (£–£££)
Corner brasserie with tables spilling out onto the side of historic Parque Colón. Barbecued chicken, salads and potatoes. A good place for morning coffee and people watching.
Parque Colón, Zona Colonial 682 6944 Daily, early until late

David Crockett (£££)
Considered the best place to eat in Santo Domingo, the president is a customer.
Gustavo Mejia Ricart 34 547 2999 Noon–midnight

Mora Pescaderia-Comedar (£–££)
Lively, noisy café serving superb fresh seafood including *lambí*, a shellfish noted for its aphrodisiac qualities. The rice and black beans, and delicious fried plantains are recommended.
Sumer Wells 22, Villa Juana 262 0257/0271 Daily until late

Museo del Jamon (££)
Not a museum but a pub with aged shanks of ham curing and hanging from its beamed ceiling. Point to the one you want and it's pulled down and sliced.
La Atarazana, Zona Colonial 688 9644 Daily until late

Palmito Gourmet (£–£££)
Serves Creole gourmet food, try a delicious goat guisado with fried plantain.
Arzobispo Portes 101, Zona Colonial 221 5777 Daily noon–11pm

Pat'e Palo Brasserie (££)
Themed restaurant with a name that means peg leg, and with waiting staff dressed as pirates. Salads, Mexican beans, fish, steak and pasta.
La Atarazana 25, Zona Colonial 687 8089 Daily, 11:30AM–1:30AM

Samurai (££–£££)
A reliable Japanese restaurant which serves excellent *sushi*.
Hector Inchaustegui Esq, Abraham Lincoln **565 1621** **Daily, lunch and evening**

Scherezade Restaurant (£–£££)
An international menu, but specialising in Mediterranean and Eastern cuisine. Also seafood and pastas.
Roberto Pastoriza 226, Naco, Santo Domingo **809 227 2323** **Daily, lunch and evening**

Restaurant Vesuvio (£££)
Smart place serving international cuisine and Caribbean food. (Also Vesuvio II at Av Tiradentes 17 – 562 6060).
Av George Washington 521 **221 3333** **Daily, 12–late**

North Coast

Restaurant Acuarela (££)
A range of international dishes are on the menu here.
Calle Professor Certad 3 , Puerto Plata **261 1000** **Tue–Sun, dinner only**

Restaurant La Carreta (£–££)
An Italian restaurant serving fish soup, lobster, salads, pizzas, pastas, seafood. Finish off with one of the very good Irish coffees or a capuccino.
17 El Batey, Sosúa **571 1217** **Daily**

La Casa del Pescador (££)
Shrimp, lobster, pastas, meats, surf 'n' turf special.
Cabarete **571 0760** **Daily until late**

Le Croissant de Paris (£)
On the busy main street, serving freshly baked pastries, ham and cheese croissants and coffee. Hectic at breakfast, though you can take away.
Cabarete **Breakfast, lunch**

Hemingway's Café (£–££)
Live rock and reggae bands perform in this popular meeting place in the shopping complex at Playa Dorada resort. The food is a familiar mix of burgers, burritos, tacos, nachos, steaks and pasta.
Playa Dorada Plaza **320 2230** **11AM–late**

Panderia Reposteria Dick (£)
On the busy main street in Cabarete and serving a range of breakfasts, German bread, pastries and coffee.
Cabarete **Breakfast, lunch**

La Puntilla de Piergiorgo (£££)
White tables trimmed with pink are set in alcoves on the cliff above the Atlantic Ocean. Very romantic atmosphere and excellent Italian food. Owned and created by the Italian designer Pier Giorgio. The menu includes seafood, meats and speciality pastas. Part of the Pier Giorgio Palace Hotel (➤ 78).
Sosúa **571 2215** **9AM–midnight**

La Rocq (££)
Local dishes including seafood specialities.
Calle Pedro Clisart, Sosua **571 3893** **Daily noon–11/12PM**

Lunch
Lunch here is the main meal of the day and the Latin tradition of a long lunch appeals. Take advantage of the fact that many shops, museums and businesses close by tucking into a sumptuous meal and then relaxing for a couple of hours siesta afterwards. Dinner is taken late, allowing you to visit the theatre or watch a baseball game first.

Opening Hours
Opening times are subject to change, so it's always wise to phone ahead. For popular restaurants reserve your table in advance.

Seafood
If there's more than one of you dining, order a seafood platter of lobster, langoustine, shrimp and other fish. Accompany this with a big salad, fried potatoes and marinated tomatoes. Add a few husks of bread and dive in.

Coping with Crabs
For getting all the flesh out of crab claws, some restaurants offer you a wooden chopping board and a hammer. Simply bash the claw and scrape out the juicy white meat.

Tipíco Bonao (££–£££)
Frequented by top executives, politicians and business people travelling the main highway. The wide range of dishes includes seafood, chicken and lobster.
Duarte Highway, between Santo Domingo and Santiago 248 7942 Daily 6AM–10PM

Ristorante Vento (£–££)
Candlelit tables on a terrace overlooking the beach or actually on the sands. Shoe-shine boys will polish your shoes for a few pesos while you dine. Salads, shrimp, lobster, meats.
Calle Principal Km. 14, Cabarete 571 0977 6AM–11PM. Closed Mon

Southeast

Capitán Cook Restaurant (£–££)
Amazing seafood restaurant actually on the soft sands of the beach. Fresh lobster, langoustine, shrimp, octopus and fish caught regularly and brought to the restaurant's coolbox, in the shape of a treasure chest. Food is fried or grilled on stoves in the open. Also pastas, chicken, steaks, salads and jugs of sangria.
Playa El Cortecito, (Entrance Hoteles Fiesta y Carabela), Nr Higüey 552 0645 Day and night

Marina Punta Cana (££–£££)
An Italian restaurant, built of wood and thatch, half of it jutting out into the Caribbean Sea, the other half on dry land. Nudging Punta Cana's marina, often occupied by a few swish yachts. Fish and shellfish, plus pastas and Italian specialities feature on the menu.
Punta Cana 221 2262 Daily, lunch and evening

Neptuno's Restaurant (££–£££)
Boasting a romantic setting with tables on a boardwalk over the lagoon and an impressive menu of fish and shellfish.
Boca Chica 523 4703 Daily, lunch and evening

La Piazetta (£££)
Italian restaurant and one among many restaurants, from Mexican to French, at Altos de Chavón.
Altos de Chavón via Casa de Campo 523 3333 ext 5339 Daily, evenings, 6–11PM

Southwest

Brisas del Caribe (£–££)
A seafront venue offering a variety of seafood, local and international dishes on the menu.
Carretera Batey Central, Baharona 524 2794 Noon–11PM

La Rocca (££)
Well known for seafood, chicken and Chinese food.
Av Enriquillo, Baharona 970 7630 Evenings only. Closed Mon

Cordillera Central

Restaurant El Rancho (££)
Fish, seafood, steaks, chicken. Specialities are chicken stuffed with sweet plantains, crêpes with seafood, watercress soup. Also pizzas and sandwiches.
Jarabacoa 574 4024/4557 Daily until late

Santo Domingo & Around the Country

Santo Domingo

Hotel Conde de Peñalba (£–££)
Hotel within a splendid colonial building in Parque Colón in the old town. Balconies overlooking the main square and the cathedral. Cafeteria-bistro with tables spilling out onto the square. Rooms have air-conditioning, telephone and television.
✉ **Arzobispo Meriño, Zona Colonial** ☎ **688 7379; fax 688 7375**

Maison Gautreaux (£)
Pleasant, budget guest house with air-conditioned rooms, friendly service, cable TV and close to Avenue George Washington and the Caribbean seafront.
✉ **Calle Felix, Mariano Lluberes No. 8, Gazcue** ☎ **687 4856/412 7837; fax 412 7840**

El Palacio (£££)
Said to be the best hotel in Santo Domingo. Situated in the old town within easy walking distance of the historic sites.
✉ **Calle Duarte** ☎ **682 4730; fax 687 5535**

Santo Domingo Hotel (££)
Big city hotel with a casino on site. Rooms come with TV, air-conditioning, mini-bar and some have balconies looking across to the Caribbean Sea.
✉ **Av Independencia** ☎ **221 1511/535 4030**

Hotel Sofitel Frances (££)
Beautiful hotel in a 16th-century building, next to the city's historical sites. Rooms have satellite TV, mini-bar and telephone. Restaurant serving French and international cuisine in colonial courtyard set around a fountain.
✉ **Calle Las Mercedes, Esq Arzobispo Meriño, Zona Colonial** ☎ **685 9331; fax 685 1289**

Santiago

Hotel Aloha Sol (££)
Smart, city centre hotel right on the main Calle Del Sol avenue which leads to many of the main attractions and the Monumento a los Héroes de la Restauración de la República. Air-conditioned, en suite rooms with TV, mini-bar. Restaurant attached.
✉ **Calle Del Sol No 51** ☎ **581 9203; fax 583 0950**

North Coast

Cacao Beach (££)
One of a few resorts mingling with European hotels in what many regard as an increasingly popular area.
✉ **Las Terrenas** ☎ **240 6000/240 6020**

Gran Ventana Beach Resort (Playa Dorada) (££)
One of at least 14 all-inclusive resorts in the Playa Dorada complex. Bigger than its sister, the Victoria Resort, and more attuned to families, the hotel comes with its own beach, numerous restaurants, supervised children's room and even babysitting at an extra charge. Beauty salon, tennis, watersports and windsurfing, sailing, *merengue* lessons and more.
✉ **PO Box 22, Puerto Plata** ☎ **320 2111; fax 320 2112**

Prices
Rates shown are during peak season, from early December to Easter. Prices are for a double room, excluding breakfast and 23 per cent tax, unless all-inclusive is stated.
£ = under US$60
££ = US$60–220
£££ = over US$220

Food
Some holidaymakers stay clear of street vendors selling everything from sugarcane juice and fried chicken to baked sweet potatoes and finger food. Others swear they evoke the true taste of the country and try the lot.

Drinkable Water
Tap water is not safe to drink. Stick to bottled water. It's your choice whether to take ice cubes in your alcohol, cocktails or fruit juices but if in doubt, go without.

Iberostar (££–£££)
Plush five-star resort, part of a well-known chain. Just 5 minutes from the nearest airport. Watersports and *merengue* lessons are some of the activities available.
Playa Dorada ☎ 320 1000

Pier Giorgio Palace Hotel (££)
Once home to the late John Bartlow Martin, writer and former US Ambassador in the Dominican Republic. Now owned by an Italian fashion designer, Pier Giorgio. A romantic, white, Victorian-style hotel with tropical gardens overlooking the Atlantic Ocean. Own restaurant with tables offering great views of the surf below (➤ 75). Five minutes from airport and boasting a limousine service.
Calle la Puntilla No 1, El Batey, Sosúa ☎ 571 2626; fax 571 2788

Puerto Plata Village (Playa Dorada) (££)
Sugar-pink and pastel-coloured chalet suites with white fancy verandas mingle with apartment blocks of rooms set among luscious tropical palm gardens. Again, this has all that one expects from an all-inclusive, including a day-long programme of activities, from aqua-shape-up to theatre shows.
PO Box 716, Puerto Plata
☎ 320 4012; fax 320 5113

San Souci Beach Apartments (£)
Self-catering apartments fronting the beach and the windsurfing action.
Cabarete ☎ 571 0613; fax 571 1542

Victoria Resort (Playa Dorada) (££)
Attractive for golfers as it features a Robert Trent Jones course, on the banks of a lily- and duck-inhabited lagoon. Own beach area reached on foot or by courtesy shuttle bus. Watersports, air-conditioned rooms and suites and a choice of restaurants.
PO Box 22, Puerto Plata
☎ 320 1200; fax 320 4862

Hotel Villa Taina (£–££)
Stylish small hotel on Cabarete's main street. Decorated with original and copy Taino artefacts. Air-conditioned rooms, balcony or terrace and breakfast on the beach.
Cabarete ☎ 571 0722; fax 571 0883

Southeast

Casa de Campo (£££)
Internationally famous and dubbed 'the Caribbean's most complete resort' – it's like a small town which you travel through on personal golf carts. Restaurants, shops and beautiful beach. Three 18-hole Pete Dye-designed golf courses including 'The Teeth of the Dog'. Also fishing, watersports, tennis, shooting and equestrian centres and polo training. New marina and yacht club being developed. With 300 hotel rooms and 150 luxury villas.
PO Box 140, La Romana
☎ 523 3333; fax 523 8000

Coral Hamaca Beach Hotel and Casino (££)
All-inclusive and the most popular in Boca Chica. Set right on its own beach and

with a number of restaurants featuring international cuisine, including Italian and Chinese.
Boca Chica 523 4611; fax 523 6767

Costa Caribe Beach Hotel and Casino (££)
All-inclusive, small and intimate hotel with daily activities, watersports and entertainment programme, including tennis, Spanish lessons, trekking, sailing, dance lessons and aqua gym. The range of restaurants include Mexican, Italian and seafood.
Juan Dolio 526 2244; fax 526 3141

Hotel Iberostar Bávaro (£££)
One of a handful of Iberostar 5-star resorts featuring spacious rooms amidst a tropical garden setting, complete with ducks, herons and peacocks. Facilities include tennis courts, a beauty salon, watersports and diving, children's programme and numerous restaurants and meals packages.
Bávaro, Higüey 221 6500; fax 688 6186

Metro Hotel Golf and Marina (££)
All inclusive, newly refurbished and very smart. Swimming pool yards from the palm beach and sea. Five minutes away from 18-hole golf course. Fishing trips, yacht and boating excursions available. Watersports include windsurfing, paddle boating and other non-motorised aquatic sport.
Apartado Postal 837, Juan Dolio 526 2811; fax 526 1808

Olimpo Hotel (£)
This nice, friendly budget hotel is situated on the main street.
Av Padre Abreu Esq Pedro A Lluberes, La Romana 550 7646; fax 550 7647

Punta Cana Resort (££)
Set on a naturally superb white beach and renowned for its attention to detail, service and food. Ocean-view rooms and new luxury golf villas with interiors designed by Dominican fashion designer, Oscar de la Renta, each with own private beach, and some with open-air jacuzzi. Golf course designed by Pete Dye. Good diving and snorkelling, ecological reserve. Own airport.
Playa Punta Cana 221 2262/687 8745

Southwest

Hotel Casa Bonita (££)
Beautifully decorated hill-top hotel, open-style chateaux overlooking Baharona and the sea.
Baharona 472 2163

Cordillera Central

Rancho Baiguate (££)
Safari-style ranch with a swimming pool backed by mountains and reached across a wooden bridge. Lunch is a typical Dominican-style buffet with organically grown vegetables and fruit. Watch the cook making the cassava bread in the traditional way. Awarded the 'Green Button' by the Ministry of Tourism. (New hotel nearby just opened.)
Jarabacoa 574 6890; fax 574 4940

Choice of Accommodation
With no fewer than 53,964 hotel rooms, the country offers a choice of places to stay, from small beach inns and hotels to colonial city hostels and those catering for adventure travel. The country is famous for its all-inclusive beach resorts which are cheaper when booked through a tour operator. Prices vary widely and can be as confusing as the combinations often available. For example, room only is much cheaper than three meals a day included, and gives you the option of trying out other restaurants. In low season, however, you may be able to turn up and book a few nights' stay. Alternatively, you might be able to buy a day pass, but check that the watersports are not fully booked. A few have a creche or kids' club where you can leave the children while you enjoy the facilities and bars.

Shopping

Shop Opening Times
Opening hours are usually 8–12 or 10–12, then 2–7 or 3–7.

Souvenirs
Carved mahogany sculptures, hand-painted masks and *merengue*-playing music boxes make great souvenirs. La Atarazana in Zona Colonial, Santo Domingo is a good place. Cheaper yet colourful items cram the beaches and main streets of Sosúa and Cabarete on the north coast. You'll also see Taino-inspired art, silver jewellery, ceramics, papier mâché, baskets, sarongs and woven hats.

Santo Domingo

The focus of shopping is El Conde in Zona Colonial, a pedestrianised street with an unusually high number of shoe shops, plus souvenirs, cheap clothing, electrical goods and cigars. The more upmarket stores have good quality cigars, rum, ceramic faceless dolls, art, *merengue* CDs and wooden African carvings. Fashion names include Versace, Nautica, Benetton, Guess, Ralph Lauren, Liz Claiborne and the popular local, Dominican fashion designer Oscar de la Renta.

Shopping Centres

Plaza Central
The country's biggest, with air-conditioned floors of banks, boutiques, furniture, ornaments, sportswear, jewellery, children's toys and clothing. Elevators and escalators rise above a central fountain to the cinema, restaurants and nightclubs at the top. You can spend all day here and there are video games to keep the children entertained. Dine out then dance the night away or watch a movie.
27 de Febrero and Winston Churchill, Santo Domingo 567 5012 Daily (some parts on Sundays, plus entertainment)

Playa Dorada Plaza
Part of the massive Playa Dorada complex of resorts on the north coast. A bright and busy place with a range of shops selling souvenirs, fashion, music and personal necessities.
Playa Dorada 320 2000
Daily 11AM–11PM

Antiques

De Soto Galeria
Paintings, furniture and pottery within an historic building.
Calle Hostos No 215, Zona Colonial, Santo Domingo
689 6109 Daily

Art and Crafts

Most of the paintings sold on the street are by artists from across the border in Haiti. Their style is noticeable for its distinctively vivid colours and abstract designs. The softer, more realistic Dominican art is usually found only in galleries. Look out especially for works by Pedro Cespedes, Carlos Puello and Marcial Baez.

De Mi Pais
A gift shop selling earrings and other jewellery in amber and larimar. Also paintings and local art, cigars and drinks.
Calle Arzobispo Meriño 164
164 689 3972

Cigars

L Tienda del Fumador
Supplying a wide selection of cigars, pipes, cigarettes, boxed gift sets and accessories.
Fco Prats Ramirez No 159, Santo Domingo 541 3390
10–2, 3–8

Fabrica de Tabacos
A well-stocked tobacco shop where you can actually see cigars being hand-rolled. There is also a museum upstairs.
Parque Colón, Zona Colonial, Santo Domingo
535 4448
9–6

Jewellery

Harrisons
A reputable jewellers with branches around the island and in several hotels. Chosen by EuroCheque as the official jewellers of the Dominican Republic. Fine jewellery of amber and larimar. Also sell Dominican black jade – 'Jadite', a hard stone but soft in appearance mined in the southwest. Harrisons say black jade offers an alternative to the endangered black coral. See them being made at the shop.
✉ Plaza Isabela, Puerto Plata ☎ 586 3933 ◷ Daily 8–6

Museo de Ambar Dominicano
Similar items for sale as in the Santo Domingo amber museum. Jewellery and souvenirs are on display in the lower floor of a beautiful white house that doubles as a highly popular amber museum (▶ 43).
✉ Calle Duarte 61, Peurta Plata ☎ 586 2848 ◷ Closed Sun

Museo Mundo de Amber
Within the town's amber museum (▶ 36). Fabulous collection of souvenirs and trinkets from inexpensive, quirky keyrings decorated with a blob of amber to pricey pieces set in silver and gold. Also a pretty selection of blue larimar.
✉ Calle Arzobispo Meriño, Zona Colonial, Santo Domingo ☎ 682 3309 ◷ 8:30–6, Sun 9–1

Supermarket

A good place to stock up on everyday necessities.
✉ La Rosada, Cabarete ☎ 571 0754 ◷ 7:30AM–8:30PM

Shopping in other Resorts

North Coast

The main *carretera* or coastal road forms a continuous corridor of tourist-oriented shops selling everything from Haitian paintings and tie-dye beachwear to souvenir ornaments. There is also much Taino-style sculptures and unusual silver jewellery.

Sosúa

As in Cabarete, the streets of Sosúa are crammed with tourist bars, restaurants and souvenir shops. You can also find smart watches and sportswear in the scuba and windsurfing shops. Towards the ocean-front is a colourful market area selling souvenirs made from coconut shells, wooden sculptures, musical instruments, *merengue* CDs, paintings, ornaments, sarongs and wacky T-shirts.
✉ Calle Duarte/Calle Pedro Clisante, Sosúa ◷ Daily until late

Boca Chica

Busy resort streets filled with typical Dominican souvenirs and Haitian paintings.
✉ Av Duarte, Boca Chica ◷ Daily until late

Altos de Chavón

There are artists' studios, a French bakery, souvenir boutiques, jewellery shops and an interior design store selling fashionable soft furnishings, all set within this reconstructed Mediterranean village (▶ 12).
✉ Near Casa de Campo resort, La Romana ☎ 523 3333 ◷ Daily until late

Music: *Merengue* and *Bachata*
Merengue is the pulsating heart of Dominican life. The country's history has found its way in recordings of this popular music that is played in streets, in cars and in homes. Noticed by a Frenchman who visited the country in 1795, *merengue* is a dance of the people's passion. It vibrates in 2:4 time to the rhythm of the *güira*, the *tambora* (small drum) and the accordion, building up power until it reaches a dramatic climax. Used by the indigenous Indians in ceremonies, the *güira* is actually a hollow brass cylinder, covered in goat's skin. When rubbed it emits a buzzing sound. *Bachata* is country music with a distinct popping rhythm and usually comes with romantic or heartbreaking lyrics.

Nightlife

Gentlemen's Clubs
Gentlemen's clubs are supposedly respectable places where men watch girls dancing and stripping, and are not allowed to touch. A popular one is Doll House (Avenue George Washington 557, Santo Domingo, 689 5301), open nightly, from 8PM, except Mondays. Membership scheme in operation.

Santo Domingo
El Boulevado, which has a new sculpture park with a wrought-iron clock tower, is a lively, neon-lit thoroughfare at night. In Zona Colonial try Plaza de la Hispanidad. Along La Atarazana reputable restaurants serve delicious food and host regular flamenco and other music performances.

El Aguila
Enjoy Salsa music every night at El Aguila. No admission charge. See the locals dance in the aisles and play instruments.
Av San Vincente de Paul 20, Los Palmas de Alma Rosa
598 1888
Nightly,from 7PM. Closes when it empties

Fridays American Bar
Admission free except Fridays and Saturdays. A wide range of music, from salsa to rap.
Acropolis Plaza **955 8443** **Day and night**

Guácara Taina
Situated in a huge bat cave. Live *merengue* and salsa makes it very busy at weekends.
Mirador Sur **536 0671**
Nightly. Closed Mon

Jet Set
Merengue music. Every Monday and Thursday a visiting *merengue* orchestra plays (entry fee).
Avenida Indepencia No 2253 **535 4145** **Nightly**

Schizo
New high class disco.
Avenue Abraham Lincoln 158 **683 3982** **Nighly from 10PM**

Trio Cafe
High-class bar where the customers arrive in Porsches.
Lincoln Ave
Nightly

Around the Country

Bávaro Disco
Famous club at Barceló Bávaro Beach Resort. If you're not a resident at the all-inclusive resort, you can always buy day and night passes.
Bávaro **686 5797**
Weekends

Club Génesis
A perfect way to end a day at this recreated medieval Mediterranean village. Ladies' and tequilla nights are popular.
Altos de Chavón
Via Casa de Campo 523 3333
Fri and Sat, 11PM–4AM

Tiki Bar
A great place for those who enjoy live music and cheap drinks.
Cabarete
Nightly

Tropicalissimo Show
Leading Latin American and Caribbean music entertainment.
Bávaro Casino, Barceló
221 6500

Folklore Shows and Theatre

Teatro Nacional
Modern building hosting opera, ballet, orchestral concerts.
Plaza de la Cultura, Santo Domingo **687 3191**
Smart dress only

Sports & Activities

Golf

Santo Domingo

Las Lagunas Country Club
18 holes, par 72.
✉ **20 Duarte Highway**
☎ **372 7441**

Isabel Villas Country Club
9 holes, par 3. Lights for night play.
✉ **Avenida Belice, Cuesta Hermosa II, Arroyo Hondo**
☎ **549 6645**

Santo Domingo Country Club
18 holes, par 72.
✉ **Calle Isabel Aguiar**
☎ **530 6606**

Around the Country

Costa Azul Golf
9 holes, par 33. Flat, sprawling 45-acre course.
✉ **Carretera Sosúa–Cabarete, Puerto Plata** ☎ **571 2608**

Golf de Bávaro
18 holes, par 72. Tropical gardens and bordering lakes.
✉ **Barceló Resorts Complex, Bávaro** ☎ **686 5797**

Jarabacoa Golf Club
9 holes, par 72. Set amidst the pine-clad alpine slopes.
✉ **Quintas de Primavera, Jarabacoa** ☎ **573 2474**

The Links
18 holes, par 72. The resort's second championship course.
✉ **Casa de Campo, La Romana**
☎ **523 8115**

Loma de Chivo Country Club
9 holes, par 3. Challenging, small course in rolling hills.
✉ **Gran Bahía Hotel, Km 8 Carretera Samaná–as Galeras, Samaná** ☎ **538 3111**

Los Marlins Golf Course
18 holes, par 72. Opened 1995. Near Juan Dolio beach.
✉ **Metro Country Club, Las Américas Highway, Juan Dolio**
☎ **526 3315**

Los Mangos Golf Course
9 holes, par 32. Course within tropical fruit trees.
✉ **Calle Principal, Costambar, Puerto Plata** ☎ **970 7143**

Playa Dorada Golf Course
18 holes, par 72. Exceptional greens and pleasant lagoon setting.
✉ **Playa Dorada, Puerto Plata**
☎ **320 3344/320 4262**

Playa Grande Golf Course
18 holes, par 72. Ten holes interact with the Caribbean Sea. Exclusive resort.
✉ **Km 6 Carretera Río San Juan–Cabrera** ☎ **248 5314**

Punta Cana Golf Course
18 holes. Also Peter B Dye's new challenge course with 14 holes and views of the Caribbean coastline.
✉ **Punta Cana** ☎ **541 2714**

San Andrés Caribe Golf Club
9 holes, par 36 and four tee positions. Near Boca Chica beach.
✉ **Km 27 Las Américas Highway, Boca Chica** ☎ **549 6645**

The Teeth of the Dog
18 holes, par 72. World-renowned championship course set on the edge of the Caribbean coastline.
✉ **Casa de Campo, La Romana**
☎ **523 8115**

Eternal Golf
Golf brings in thousands of tourists to the Dominican Republic. Summer weather all year round and a climate that makes playing in rainy days seem enjoyable are not the only draws: internationally famous architects have designed courses to rival anywhere in the world and test the skills of golfers, both beginners and advanced.
Tournament information from Association of Golf ☎ 476 4541/4898

Diving
In the southeast, around Isla Saona and Isla Catalina, are reefs with unusually shaped sponges and thousands of fish. Visibility is often more than 50m. Catalina Island is known for its wall where barracudas, eagle rays and mourays congregate. El Toro reef, also near Saona, is a favourite place for nurse sharks. Parque Nacional Submarine La Caleta is where to dive the wreck, *The Hickory*. Hotspots in the north include the massive coral reef, Silver Banks, near Puerto Plata, and the Bahía de Samaná.

Wet Fun in Boca Chica
Playa Boca Chica (► 20, Top Ten) is a calm, natural swimming pool protected by a reef and is therefore ideal for children. Aside from swimming and playing on the sands, you can go yachting, snorkelling, scuba diving or ride the banana boat.

Baseball
The season runs from October to January. The main venues are in Santo Domingo and San Pedro de Macoris. Contact Ligue de Baseball:
566 9696
or
The National Stadium for Baseball
Santo Domingo **732 3014**

Bowling
Punta Cana Lane
New championship alley, opened 2002.
959 4444

Children's Activities

Acuarío Nacional
The island's aquarium has turtles, sharks, stingrays and, the newest acquisition, a manatee.
Av 28 de Enero, Santo Domingo **766 1709**
Tue–Sun 9:30–5:30

Columbus Aquapark
Cabarete
571 2742
Daily 10–6

Parque Zoológico Nacional
A miniature railway transports you round a mixed gathering of African wildlife (including tigers), flamingos, native and colourful birds and creatures in the children's zoo.
Av los Reyes Católicos, Santo Domingo **562 3149**
Tue–Sat, 9–6

Deep Sea Fishing
Sea trips guided by professional instructors. Equipment provided.
523 4511

Horse Riding

Iguana Mama
Rides through sugarcane fields, along back roads, and on beach.
Cabarete
571 0908

Godin Tours
Multilingual guides and Criollo horses. Rides through the countryside and featuring swimming and the tastings of tropical fruits and local rum.
Rancho Montaña
248 5407

Mountain biking

Iguana Mama
Half- and full-day mountain descents. Features include swimming, and a look at Dominican culture, vegetation and food. Mountain bikes, helmets, water and support vehicle are provided.
Cabarete
571 0908

Multi-adventure Activities

Adventure Riding Park
Facilities for rallying, horse riding, shooting and off-road-driving. English- , Spanish- and German-speaking guides.
Río San Juan
396 3220

Maxim Aventura
Adventure centre in the foothills of the Dominican Alps including rock climbing, volleyball, basketball, birdwatching, horse riding, quadbikes, jeep safaris, rafting on the Río Yaque del Norte, canyoning and

mountain biking.
Rancho Baiguate, Jarabacoa 574 6890

Polo
Tuition and matches held at Casa de Campo resort.
La Romana, Altos de Chavón 523 3333

Scuba Diving
PADI courses, from beginner to advanced. Dive excursions, night dives, wreck dives and drive dives available.

Padi Dive Centre Viva Diving
Bayahibe 686 5658

Northern Coast Diving
Calle Pedtro Clisante 8, Sosúa 571 1028

Tours & Excursions

Caribbean Bike and Adventure
Cycling, family adventures, whale-watching, mule trekking. Plus multi-sport activities combining, for example, cycling and horseback riding. Canyoning, rock climbing and scuba diving are also popular,
Cabarete 571 1748

Splish Splash
Tours by catarmaran and speedboat around Parque Nacional del Este and Saona Island.
Bahayibe/Saona 349 6930

Turinter Tour Operator
Tours to Punta Cana, Saona Island, Isla Catalina, Puerto Plata. In fact just about the whole of the island.
Santo Domingo 686 4020

Trekking
Excursions of 3, 4 and 5 days to Pico Duarte and other peaks. Includes overnight camping and traditional Dominican cooking.

Maxim Aventura
Rancho Baiguate, Jarabacoa 574 6890

Iguana Mama
Cabarete 571 0908

Whale-watching

Iguana Mama
Cabarete 571 0908

Whale Samoná Victoria Marine
538 2588

Windsurfing and Kiteboarding
Cabarete is the top resort for windsurfing and kiteboarding practice and tuition, for both beginners and experienced. Equipment is available for hire.

Carib Bic Centre
571 0640

Club Mistral
571 0582 (ext 23)

The Olympic Park (Sports Palace)
Bounded by four streets, and used for the 2003 Pan American Olympic Games. The park has facilities for basketball, softball, an Aquatics Center, velodrome, Combat Pavilion and Volleyball Pavilion.
Avenue Ortega y Gasset/ Avenida 27 de Febrero, Santo Domingo

Children in the Sun
Small children are particularly vulnerable to the sun and their skin needs to be well protected. Apply a high-factor sunblock regularly, especially after swimming.

What's On When

Carnivals
Carnivals were first introduced by the Spanish, and influenced by the African slaves. Today nearly every town in the country has its own fiesta or homage to a patron saint. Multiple-horned masks, vibrantly painted, are worn to drive out evil spirits, and both costume and mask vary with the region. In Santiago, for instance, 'devils' in masks carry pig's bladders which look like balloons and they use them to bash you playfully over the head. Children, especially, dress as jesters, their shiny jumpsuits decorated with bells or mirrors.

January
21 Jan: *Virgin of La Altagracia day*. This is a major pilgrimage to Basílica de Nuestra Señora de la Altagracia in Higüey, where the Virgin Mary supposedly appeared in 1691 (and many times since).
26 Jan: *Juan Pablo Duarte's birthday*. Carnival fever grips the country, leading up to National Independence Day celebrations (February).

February
27 Feb (or last Sunday of the month): *National Independence Day* is a massive holiday celebrating the day in 1844 when Juan Pablo Duarte, Francisco del Rosario Sánchez and Ramón Matías Mella overthrew the occupying Haitians. Raising the three-coloured flag of the nation (navy, red and white) they declared independence at Puerto del Conde (Gate of Entrance) in El Conde street, in the historic Zona Colonial. Celebrations usually begin on 26 Jan, birthday of Duarte, and continue to the big day. If you're there, head down to Av George Washington in Santo Domingo. Locals form a corridor between the seafront and the city and through it parade representatives of the country's national fighting force, from commandos to fighter pilots. Police squads and troops, together with tanks, guns and military vehicles, pass in front of the president, while aircraft drop parachutists in a dramatic finale.
The northwest town of Monte Cristi hosts the *El Morro* Carnival featuring a person acting as an evil, angry bull who has a mock battle with the good civilians. People dance in the street, eat, drink and later consume quantities of sugarcane juice to relieve their hangovers.

June
In Puerto Plata, at the foot of Fuerte San Felipe, a week-long Cultural Festival is held featuring blues, jazz, salsa and *merengue*. Dancers and musicians from around the country drop by to perform to the excited crowds.
The Cabarete Race Week (an international windsurfing competition) each June.

July
Third week: A notable *merengue* festival erupts along the *malécon* (seafront) in Santo Domingo. Singers and dancers compete for prizes for the best live performances. The festival is so popular it has now extended to Boca Chica.

August
16 Aug: *Restoration Day*, marking the country's declaration of war with Spain in 1863. Yet another hectic carnival with elaborate floats and *merengue* dancing.

October
Puerto Plata's contribution to *merengue* takes off with a festival that smothers the *malécon* with stalls, hot food, beer and festivities.
Jazz festival around Sosúa and Cabarete.

December
Early Dec–6 Jan: Christmas parties most weekends. Tree branches are painted green and white and decorated with ornaments.

Practical Matters

Before You Go 88
When You Are There 89
Language 92

Above: *be stylish and have your hair braided whilst sunning on Playa Dorada Beach*
Right: *a public telephone in the Dominican Republic*

TIME DIFFERENCES

GMT	Dominican Republic	Germany	USA (NY)	Netherlands	Spain
12 noon	8AM ←	1PM →	7AM ←	1PM →	1PM →

BEFORE YOU GO

WHAT YOU NEED

● Required
○ Suggested
▲ Not required

Some countries require a passport to remain valid for a minimum period (usually at least six months) beyond the date of entry – contact their consulate or embassy or your travel agent for details.

	UK	Germany	USA	Netherlands	Spain
Passport (for stay of less than 90 days)	●	●	●	●	●
Tourist card (US$10 payable on arrival)	●	●	●	●	●
Onward or return ticket	▲	▲	▲	▲	▲
Health inoculations (polio, tetanus, typhoid, hepatitis A)	○	○	○	○	○
Health documentation (➤ 91, Health)	▲	▲	▲	▲	▲
Travel insurance	○	○	○	○	○
Driving licence (national with Spanish translation or international)	●	●	●	●	●
Car insurance certificate	○	○	○	○	○
Car registration document	n/a	n/a	n/a	n/a	n/a

WHEN TO GO

Dominican Republic

High season

Low season (Note: September–October is the hurricane season)

	JAN	FEB	MAR	APR	MAY	JUN	JUL	AUG	SEP	OCT	NOV	DEC
Season	High	High	High	High	Low	Low	Low	Low	Low	Low	Low	High
Temperature	25°C	25°C	25°C	25°C	25°C	28°C	28°C	28°C	28°C	28°C	25°C	26°C
Weather	Sun	Sun	Sun	Sun/showers	Wet	Wet	Wet	Sun/showers	Sun/showers	Sun/showers	Sun	Sun

Sun · Sun/showers · Wet

TOURIST OFFICES

In the UK
18/22 Hand Court
High Holborn
London
WC1V 6JE
☎ 020 7242 7778
Fax: 020 7405 4202

In the USA
E 57th Street, Suite 803
136 New York
NY 10022
Toll Free 1 888 374 6361
☎ 212 588 1012/13/14
Fax: 212 588 1015

EMBASSIES AND CONSULATES

UK	Germany	USA	Spain
472 7111	565 8811	221 2171	535 1615

WHEN YOU ARE THERE

ARRIVING

Both scheduled and charter flights arrive at the country's eight international airports. Major airlines include Air Canada, Air France, American Airlines, British Airways, Aerolineas Argentinas and Iberia. Arrival by sea is by cruise liner only. Before entering the country, the regulatory international form should be filled out to give to immigration authorities on arrival.

MONEY

The Dominican monetary unit is the peso (RD$) divided into 100 centavos. Foreign currency can be changed at exchange booths of the Banco de Reservas at airports, major hotels or commercial banks. Banking hours are 8:30AM to 4PM, Monday to Friday. Some banking branches remain open until 9PM on Saturday and Sunday mornings. Airport booths remain open to service all incoming flights, up to 24 hours if necessary. Travellers' cheques and major credit cards are widely accepted. Cash advances are available at some commercial banks.

CUSTOMS

YES

2 litres of alcoholic liquor
200 cigarettes
gift articles to the value of US$1,000

NO

Drugs, firearms, ammunition, offensive weapons, obscene material, unlicensed animals.

OPENING HOURS

- Shops
- Offices
- Banks
- Attractions/museums
- Post offices
- Pharmacies

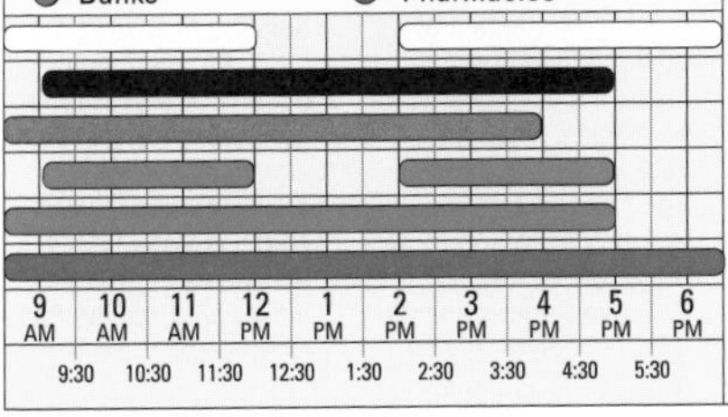

Some shops usually close Saturday at 2PM. Major stores are also open on Sundays until 2PM, some until 10PM. Consulates and embassies are open 8–2. Churches hold weekly services (Santo Domingo's synagogue Friday evenings). There are 24-hr pharmacies in Santo Domingo and some other major cities.

POLICE 911

TOURIST POLICE 1 200 3500

FIRE 911

AMBULANCE 911

DRIVE ON THE **RIGHT**

TOILETS **FREE**

DRIVING

Speed limit on motorways: **80 or 100kph**

Speed limit on main roads: **60kph**

Speed limit on minor roads: **40kph**

Legally required, although you'll see the locals without them. Unsurfaced roads and manic drivers make the Dominican Republic a hazardous place to drive. Exercise caution at all times and always wear a seat belt, regardless of what anyone else is doing. Beware of corrupt domestic traffic police that have a habit of stopping you for a dubious offence, demanding an on-the-spot fine. Driving by night should be avoided.

Although there are no specific limits on drinking and driving, you should always drive with due care and attention. You may find that your insurance cover is not valid for accidents due to alcohol.

Service stations (*bombas*) are open until 6PM or in larger towns 10PM. The main resorts and towns have 24hr service stations but might be closed on Sundays. Petrol prices fluctuate widely. Fuel (*gasolina*) is available in diesel, unleaded, regular and regular supreme.

PUBLIC TRANSPORT

Internal Flights
Air Santo Domingo is a local airline that operates regular scheduled flights between the principal tourist regions of the country: Las Américas Dr JFPG (Santo Domingo); Herrera (Santo Domingo); Gregorio Luperón (Puerto Plata); Arroyo Barril (Samaná); Cibao (Santiago); María Montez (Barahona); Punta Aguila (Romana); Punta Cana (Higüey). Reservations ☎ 683 8020

Buses
Two bus companies, Metro Tours ☎ 566 7126 and Caribe Tours ☎ 221 4422 provide excellent transportation between Santo Domingo and major cities. Tickets are exceptionally cheap and buses are modern and comfortable with air-conditioning, drinks and sweets. Passengers are recommended to book seats in advance.

Gua-guas
A type of mini bus, the *gua-gua* trundles between the country's smaller towns, resorts and historic sites and is usually weighed down with both locals and tourists. Either board them in the central squares of towns and villages or hail them down at the roadside. The low fare is usually paid at your drop-off stop.

CAR RENTAL

As a last resort, rather than use the safer buses and organised tours, you can hire a car (21+). Major car rental companies have airport and city locations. A valid driver's licence and major credit car is required. When hiring a rental car, check and double check the insurance regulations. An accident can be a very costly business and if you're a foreigner you may have problems proving your case.
To leave Santo Domingo drivers have to pay 15 pesos at exit points.

TAXIS

Private taxis are available 24 hours a day in Santo Domingo, Santiago and Puerto Plata and the larger hotels. Public taxis (*carros públicos*) are similar to *gua-guas* and have to be signalled to stop. Spotlessly clean cream taxis are seen hanging around tourist sites. Although more expensive they offer a comfortable sightseeing alternative. Many drivers speak English. There are no meters, just set rates, so you must negotiate the fare in advance.

PHOTOGRAPHY

What to photograph: Dominicans are usually quite happy for you to take their photographs, but be sure to ask politely first. The mountains provide a fantastic backdrop and the beaches provide you with dramatic sunsets.
Restrictions: airports, police, army and government buildings and in banks.
When to photograph: early morning, just after sunset and late afternoon.
Where to buy film: although shops in Santo Domingo stock many types of film, you're better off bringing your own. Remember to pack spare batteries. Take film home to be developed, packing it in your carry-on bag.

TIPS/GRATUITIES

Yes ✓ No ✕		
Restaurants (service not included)	✓	10%
Cafés/bars (service not included)	✓	10%
Tour guides	✓	50 pesos
Hairdressers	✓	20 pesos
Taxis	✓	30 pesos
Chambermaids	✓	change
Porters	✕	20 pesos
Toilets	✓	change

HEALTH

Doctors
A doctor is on call at major hotels. These are stocked with medicine for the most common ailments. Ambulances are available, as is air ambulance evacuation ☎ 911.

Dental Services
Emergency dental treatment can be provided.

Sun Advice
The Caribbean sun is extremely strong and you must protect your skin. Choose a good-quality, high-factor sunscreen and reapply frequently, especially after swimming and watersports. Avoid the midday sun. Wear good sunglasses and, if possible, a wide-brimmed hat. Limit yourself when first going to the beach. If you do suffer sunburn, stay out of the sun until you recover. If symptoms of headache, nausea or dizzyness occur, call a doctor.

Drugs
Many pharmacies in Santo Domingo are open 24hrs a day. Other pharmacies are located in most cities, towns and villages. Many drugs, including antibiotics, are available without prescription.

Safe Water
Do not drink tap water. Buy bottled water for drinking and brushing teeth and check the seal is not broken. If you are unsure about ice in your drinks, go without. Never buy ice or cups of drinking water from a street vendor.

PERSONAL SAFETY

Store travel documents and valuables in your room or hotel safe. Avoid isolated streets and unfamiliar neighbourhoods, especially at night. Avoid driving at night. Beware of black market currency, drugs and prostitution in the major holiday centres. Police: ☎ 911

TELEPHONES

You can make any calls from Codetel or Tricom centres in major towns and resorts, usually open from 8AM–10PM. Pay at the counter after your call, credit cards accepted. Telephone boxes accept 25 centavo coins. Direct dial to the Dominican Republic using area code 809.

International Dialling Codes

From Dominican Republic to	
UK:	**00 11 44**
Germany:	**0 11 49**
USA and Canada:	**0 11 1**
Netherlands:	**00 11 31**
Spain	**00 11 34**

POST

Though international mail is cheap, the postal service is slow and unreliable. For parcels or documents, choose a reliable courier.

ELECTRICITY

Power supply: 110 volts/60 cycles, the same as in the US. Europeans will need an adaptor. Power cuts are not uncommon.

WHEN DEPARTING

- Visitors must pay a US$10 departure tax at the airport and must present the portion of their tourist card which they purchased on arrival.

LANGUAGE

Spanish is the official language. English is widely spoken, especially in tourist areas. Knowledge of German, Italian and French is becoming more widespread. Traffic signs and most menus in restaurants are in Spanish, although menus in tourist regions tend to be multilingual.

hotel	*hotel*	room service	*servicio de habitaciones*
bed and breakfast	*pensión*	bath	*baño*
single room	*cuarto sencillo*	shower	*ducha/regadera*
double room	*cuarto doble*	toilet	*sanitario/baño*
one person	*una persona*	balcony	*balcón*
one night	*una noche*	key	*llave*
reservation	*reserva*	lift	*levantar*
chambermaid	*camarera*	sea view	*vista mar*

bank	*banco*	credit card	*tarjeta de crédito*
exchange office	*casa de cambio*	cheque	*cheque*
post office	*el correo*	commission	*tipo de cambio*
coin	*moneda*	charge	
banknote	*billete de nanco*	cashier	*cajero*
travellers' cheques	*cheque de viajero*	change	*suelto/dinero*
exchange rate	*comisión*	foreign currency	*moneda*

café	*café*	starter	*entrada*
pub/bar	*bar*	main course	*plato principales*
breakfast	*desayuno*	dessert	*postre*
lunch	*almuerzo*	bill	*la cuenta*
dinner	*comida/cena*	beer	*cerveza*
table	*mesa*	wine	*vino*
waiter	*camarero*	water	*agua*
waitress	*camarera*		

aeroplane	*avión*	single ticket	*billete solo*
airport	*aeropuerto*	return ticket	*de ida y vuelta*
train	*ferrocarril*	non-smoking	*prohibido fumar*
bus	*autobus*	petrol	*gasolina*
bus station	*estación/terminal*	bus stop	*parada del autobus*
boat	*barco*	today	*hoy*
port	*puerto*	tomorrow	*mañana*
ticket	*boleto*		

yes	*sí*	excuse me	*perdóneme*
no	*no*	how are you?	*¿cómo está?*
please	*por favor*	do you speak English?	*¿habla usted inglés?*
thank you	*gracias*	I don't understand	*no entiendo*
you're welcome	*de nada*	how much?	*¿cuánto?*
hello	*hola*	open	*abierto*
goodbye	*adiós*	closed	*cerrar*
good morning	*buenos dias*	where is...?	*¿dónde está...?*
good afternoon	*buenos tardes*		
goodnight	*buenos noches*		

INDEX

accommodation 77–79
Acuarío Nacional 28, 84
airports and air services 89, 90
Altar de la Patria 28
Altar of the Nation 28
Altos de Chavón 12, 60
amber 36, 43
Amber Coast 44
Amber Museum 36, 81
Armando Bermúdez National Park 71
arts and crafts 80
Azua de Compostela 64

Bahía de Samaná 13
Baní 64
banks 89
Barahona 65
Basílica de Nuestra Señora de La Altagracia 56
Bávaro 57
Bayahibe 39, 57
beaches 39
bird life 9, 39, 66
boat trips
Isla Saona 60
Lago Enriquillo 68
Boca de Chavón 60
buses 90

Cabarete 7, 39, 41
Cabritos Island 65, 68
Café La Joya factory 71
car rental 90
carnivals 86
Casa de Campo 58
Casa de Máximo Gómez 64
Castillo de Cerro 67
Catedral Basílica Menor de Santa Marie, Primada de América 29
Catedral Santiago Apòstol 52
caves 45, 59, 67
Cayo Levantado 13, 39, 42, 55
children's activities 84
Church of St Stanislaus 12
Cibao Valley 52
cigars 7, 49, 80
climate and seasons 88
Coconut Coast 57
coffee 71
Columbus, Christopher 10, 16, 19, 21, 29, 30, 37
Columbus, Diego 29, 31
Columbus Park 27, 37
Constanza 70
Cordillera Central 9, 14–15, 70–71
Costa del Coco 57
credit cards 89
crocodiles 17, 39
customs reglations 89

dental services 91
departure information 92
diving 84, 85
Dominican Alps 9, 14–15, 70–71
Dominican Amber Museum 43, 81
Drake, Sir Francis 10, 29
drinking water 76, 91
drives
Amber Coast 44
jeep safari 72
Lago Enriquillo 68
driving 88, 90
drugs and medicines 91

eating out 38, 74–76
El Limón 53
El Portillo 53
electricity 91
embassies and consulates 89
emergency telephone numbers 90
entertainment 82–86

Faro a Colón 30–31
festivals and events 86
fishing 84, 85
food and drink 48–49
see also eating out
Fortaleza Ozama 31
Fortress of Santo Domingo 31
Fuerte de San Felipe 42

golf 83
Gri-Gri Lagoon 42
gua-guas (mini buses) 90

health 88, 91
helicopter tours 84
Heroes' Monument 18
Higüey 56
history 8
horse riding 84
House of Columbus 31

iguanas 17, 39
Independence Day 27
insurance 88
Isla Cabritos 65, 68
Isla de Cayo Levantado 13, 39, 42, 55
Isla Saona 7, 16, 39, 60

Jarabacoa 71
Jaragua National Park 9, 66
Jardín Botánico Nacional Rafael Moscoso 9
jeep safari 72
Jimaní 68
José del Carmen Ramírez National Park 71
José Maria Cave 59

La Descubierto 68
La Isabela National Park 19
La Romana 58
La Salinas 64
Lago Enriquillo 7, 17, 68
Laguna Gri-Gri 42
Lake Enriquillo 7, 17, 68
language 92
larimar 41, 43
Las Terrenas 53
Lighthouse to Columbus 30
local knowledge 38
local taxes 74
Los Carritas 68
Los Haïtises National Park 9, 45
Luperón Park 43

manatees 9, 39
maps
Dominican Republic 24–25
Santo Domingo 33
Maritime Museum 32
medical treatment 91
merengue 7, 38, 82
Monasterio de San Francisco 34
money 89
Monte Cristi National Park 9, 45
Monumento a los Héroes 18
mountain biking 84
multi-adventure activities 84–85
Museo Alcázar de Colón 34
Museo de Ambar Dominicano 43, 81
Museo de las Atarazanas 34
Museo La Casas Reales 35
Museo del Hombre Dominicano 35
Museo Mundo de Ambar 36, 81
Museo Nacional de Historia y Geográfia 36
Museo del Tabaco 52
Museum of the Dominican Man 35
Museum of the Royal Houses 32

National Aquarium 28, 84
National Botanic Gardens 9
National History and Geography Museum 36
National Palace 36
National Pantheon 37
National Park of the East 9, 16, 59
national parks 9
nightclubs and bars 82

opening hours 75, 89

Palacio de Borgellá 37
Palacio Nacional 36
Panteón Nacional 37
Parque Colón 27, 37
Parque Luperón 43
Parque Nacional Armando Bermúdez 71
Parque Nacional del Este 9, 16, 59
Parque Nacional Isla Cabritos 65
Parque Nacional Jaragua 9, 66
Parque Nacional José del

Carmen Ramírez 71
Parque Nacional La Isabela 19
Parque Nacional Los Haïtises 9, 45
Parque Nacional Monte Cristi 9, 45
Parque Nacional Sierra de Baoruco 66
Parque Nacional Submarino La Caleta 59
Parque Zoológico Nacional 84
passports and visas 88
personal safety 91
pharmacies 89, 91
photography 91
Pico Duarte 7, 14–15
Pico Isabel de Torres 47
Playa Boca Chica 20, 39
Playa Bonita 53
Playa Dorada 39, 47
Playa Grande 39, 47
Playa San Rafael 39, 66
police 90
polo 57, 85
postal services 89, 91
public transport 90
Puerto Plata 21, 50
Punta Cana 5, 6, 39, 63

Reserva Antropológica Cuevas de El Pomier 67
Río Chavón 60
Río Jimenoa 72
Río Yaque del Norte 6, 14, 71
Ruinas del Hospital San Nicolás de Bari 37

Salto de Baiguate 71
Salto de Caloda 53
Salto de Jimenoa 15, 71
Samana Bay 13
San Cristóbal 67
San Felipe Fort 42
San Pedro de Macorís 63
Sánta Barbara de Samana 13
Santiago de los Caballeros 18, 52
Santo Domingo 7, 22, 26–37
Saona Island 7, 16, 39, 60
shopping 80–81, 89
Sierra de Baoruco National Park 66
Sociedad Centro de Recreo 52
Sosa, Sammy 10, 63
Sosúa 39, 44, 53
Soto Galeria 34
souvenirs 80
sport and leisure 38–39, 83–85
Submarino La Caleta National Park 59
sulphur springs 68
sun advice 85, 91
Taino Indians 8, 62
taxis 90
telephones 91
time differences 88
tipping 74, 91
Tobacco Museum 52
toilets 90
Torre del Homenaje 31
tourist offices 88
tours and excursions 85
Tower of Homage 31
travel documents 88
trekking 85
Trujillo, Rafael 8, 14–15, 18, 30, 36, 53, 67

Valle Cibao 52

walks
  Manatí Park 62
  Puerta Plata 50
  Zona Colonial, Santo Domingo 32
whale-watching 7, 13, 39, 54–55, 85
wildlife 39
windsurfing 41, 85

Zona Colonial, Santo Domingo 7, 22, 32

Acknowledgements
The Automobile Association would like to thank the following photographers and libraries for their assistance in the preparation of this book:

ALLSPORT UK LTD 10; ART DIRECTORS AND TRIP PHOTO LIBRARY 28/29; BRUCE COLEMAN COLLECTION 9b, 13b, 66b; MARY EVANS PICTURE LIBRARY 8b, 10b; INTERNATIONAL PHOTOBANK 1, 5b, 7c, 21b, 23a, 38b, 39b, 48b, 53; NATURE PHOTOGRAPHERS LTD 55 (P Sterry); SPECTRUM COLOUR LIBRARY 23b

The remaining photographs are held in the Association's own library (AA PHOTOLIBRARY) and were taken by LEE KAREN STOW with the exception of 62 and 71 which were taken by CLIVE SAWYER.

Copy editor: Nick Reynolds **Page layout:** Mike Preedy
Editorial management: Pam Stagg

Dear Essential Traveller

Your comments, opinions and recommendations are very important to us. So please help us to improve our travel guides by taking a few minutes to complete this simple questionnaire.

You do not need a stamp (unless posted outside the UK). If you do not want to cut this page from your guide, then photocopy it or write your answers on a plain sheet of paper.

Send to: **The Editor, AA World Travel Guides, FREEPOST SCE 4598, Basingstoke RG21 4GY.**

Your recommendations...

We always encourage readers' recommendations for restaurants, nightlife or shopping – if your recommendation is used in the next edition of the guide, we will send you a ***FREE* AA *Essential* Guide** of your choice. Please state below the establishment name, location and your reasons for recommending it.

____

____

____

____

Please send me **AA *Essential*** ________________________

(see list of titles inside the front cover)

About this guide...

Which title did you buy?

AA *Essential* __________________________________

Where did you buy it?________________________________

When? m m / y y

Why did you choose an AA *Essential* Guide?__________________

____

____

____

____

Did this guide meet your expectations?

Exceeded ☐ Met all ☐ Met most ☐ Fell below ☐

Please give your reasons_____________________________

____

____

____

continued on next page...

Were there any aspects of this guide that you particularly liked? ________

____

____

____

Is there anything we could have done better? ________

____

____

____

____

About you...

Name (*Mr/Mrs/Ms*) ______________________________

Address ______________________________

____

______________ Postcode ______________

Daytime tel nos ______________________________

Which age group are you in?

Under 25 ☐ 25–34 ☐ 35–44 ☐ 45–54 ☐ 55–64 ☐ 65+ ☐

How many trips do you make a year?

Less than one ☐ One ☐ Two ☐ Three or more ☐

Are you an AA member? Yes ☐ No ☐

About your trip...

When did you book? m m / y y When did you travel? m m / y y

How long did you stay? ______________________________

Was it for business or leisure? ______________________________

Did you buy any other travel guides for your trip?

If yes, which ones? ______________________________

____

Thank you for taking the time to complete this questionnaire. Please send it to us as soon as possible, and remember, you do not need a stamp (*unless posted outside the UK*).

Happy Holidays!

The AA and the Automobile Association Limited, their subsidiaries and any other companies or bodies in which either has an interest ('the AA Group') may use information about you to provide you with details of other products and services, by telephone or in writing. The AA Group as a matter of policy does not release its lists to third parties.

If you do not wish to receive further information please tick the box... ☐

Dual carriageway with motorway characteristics with junction
Autobahnähnliche Schnellstraße mit Anschlussstelle

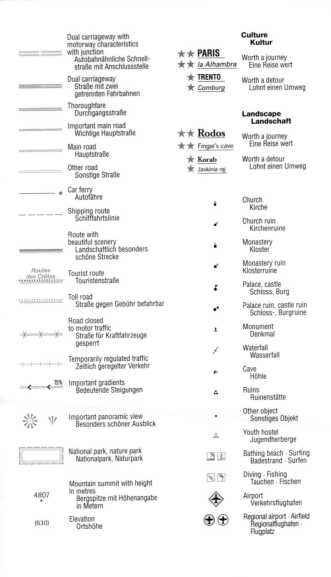

Dual carriageway
Straße mit zwei getrennten Fahrbahnen

Thoroughfare
Durchgangsstraße

Important main road
Wichtige Hauptstraße

Main road
Hauptstraße

Other road
Sonstige Straße

Car ferry
Autofähre

Shipping route
Schifffahrtslinie

Route with beautiful scenery
Landschaftlich besonders schöne Strecke

Routes des Crêtes — Tourist route
Touristenstraße

Toll road
Straße gegen Gebühr befahrbar

Road closed to motor traffic
Straße für Kraftfahrzeuge gesperrt

Temporarily regulated traffic
Zeitlich geregelter Verkehr

15% — Important gradients
Bedeutende Steigungen

Important panoramic view
Besonders schöner Ausblick

National park, nature park
Nationalpark, Naturpark

4807 — Mountain summit with height in metres
Bergspitze mit Höhenangabe in Metern

(630) — Elevation
Ortshöhe

Culture
Kultur

★★ PARIS, ★★ *la Alhambra* — Worth a journey
Eine Reise wert

★ TRENTO, ★ *Comburg* — Worth a detour
Lohnt einen Umweg

Landscape
Landschaft

★★ Rodos, ★★ *Fingal's cave* — Worth a journey
Eine Reise wert

★ Korab, ★ *Jaskinia raj* — Worth a detour
Lohnt einen Umweg

Church
Kirche

Church ruin
Kirchenruine

Monastery
Kloster

Monastery ruin
Klosterruine

Palace, castle
Schloss, Burg

Palace ruin, castle ruin
Schloss-, Burgruine

Monument
Denkmal

Waterfall
Wasserfall

Cave
Höhle

Ruins
Ruinenstätte

Other object
Sonstiges Objekt

Youth hostel
Jugendherberge

Bathing beach · Surfing
Badestrand · Surfen

Diving · Fishing
Tauchen · Fischen

Airport
Verkehrsflughafen

Regional airport · Airfield
Regionalflughafen · Flugplatz

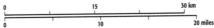

0 — 15 — 30 km
0 — 10 — 20 miles

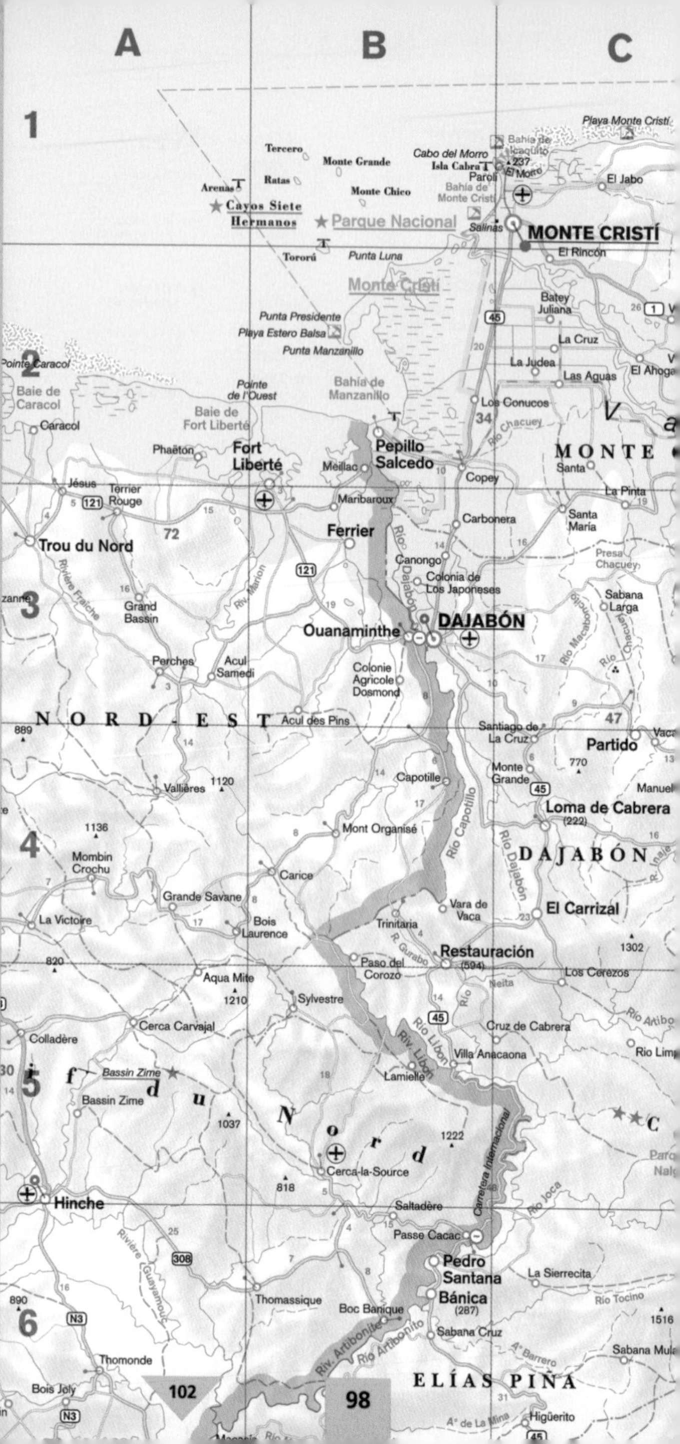
A
B
C
1
2
3
4
5
6
Playa Monte Cristi
Bahía de Icaquito
Cabo del Morro
Isla Cabra
El Morro
Paroli
237
Tercero
Monte Grande
Ratas
Monte Chico
Arenas
Cayos Siete Hermanos
Bahía de Monte Cristi
Parque Nacional
Monte Cristi
Salinas
MONTE CRISTÍ
El Jabo
El Rincón
Tororú
Punta Luna
Punta Presidente
Playa Estero Balsa
Punta Manzanillo
Batey Juliana
La Cruz
La Judea
Las Aguas
El Ahoga
Pointe Caracol
Baie de Caracol
Caracol
Pointe de l'Ouest
Bahía de Manzanillo
Baie de Fort Liberté
Los Conucos
Río Chacuey
Phaëton
Fort Liberté
Meillac
Pepillo Salcedo
Copey
MONTE
Santa
La Pinta
Jésus
Terrier Rouge
Maribaroux
Carbonera
Santa María
Trou du Nord
Ferrier
Canongo
Colonia de Los Japoneses
Presa Chacuey
Río Dajabón
Riv. Marion
Rivière Fraîche
Grand Bassin
Sabana Larga
Río Macabón
Río Chacuey
Ouanaminthe
DAJABÓN
Perches
Acul Samedi
Colonie Agricole Dosmond
NORD-EST
Acul des Pins
Santiago de La Cruz
Partido
889
Monte Grande
770
Vallières
1120
Capotille
Manuel
Loma de Cabrera
(222)
1136
Mont Organisé
Río Capotillo
Río Dajabón
DAJABÓN
Mombin Crochu
Carice
Grande Savane
Vara de Vaca
El Carrizal
La Victoire
Bois Laurence
Trinitaria
R. Gurabo
Restauración
(594)
1302
820
Paso del Corozo
Los Cerezos
Aqua Mite
1210
Sylvestre
Neita
Cerca Carvajal
Río Artibonito
Colladère
Riv. Libon
Río Libon
Cruz de Cabrera
Villa Anacaona
Rio Limp
Bassin Zime
Lamielle
Bassin Zime
Nord
1037
1222
818
Cerca-la-Source
Carretera Internacional
Hinche
Saltadère
Río Joca
Passe Cacao
Rivière Guayamouc
Pedro Santana
La Sierrecita
890
Thomassique
Bánica
(287)
Río Tocino
Boc Banique
1516
Sabana Cruz
Sabana Mula
Thomonde
Riv. Artibonite
Río Artibonito
A° Barrero
ELÍAS PIÑA
Bois Joly
102
98
A° de La Mina
Higüerito
72
34
47
45
121
N3
308

D
E
F
1
2
3
4
5
6
Cabo Isabela
Ruinas de la Isabela
29
Punta del Castillo
Parque Histórico
La Isabela
Bahía de Luperón o de Gracias
Playa Grande de Luperón
Bahía de La Isabela
El Castillo
Puente en construcción
Luperón
(4)
Punta Rucia
Cacao
Puerto Juanita
Estero Hondo
Punta Rucia
Parque Nacional Estero Hondo
Las Lagunas
R. Bajabonico
La Sabana
30
Sabana Cruz
432
El Copey
Estero Hondo
La Isabela
Unijica
El Higo
Marisol
Las Cañas
El Papayo
Alto del Papayo
403
Loma Solimán
822
A° La Jaiba
Unijica
El Mamey
Caonao
Río Caonao
Gualete
Los Hidalgos
Reserva Científica Villa Elisa
Cda de Bernardo
Vásquez
Botoncillo
Villa Sinda
Juan Gómez
1
14
Hato del Medio Arriba
A° Agua de Luis
Ranchete
17
La Caya
Marmolejos
Guananico
Cordillera Septentrional
Villa Elisa
15
Río
Guayubín
La Guajaca
Jaibón
Hatillo Palma
24
Damajagua
Cerro Gordo
20
49
Laguna Salada
Maizal
Jicomé Arriba
22
Yaque del Norte
Cana
VALVERDE
Piloto
11
1
164
Martín García
Esperanza
Pontón
31
32
Río Cana
20
Hatigo
MAO
18
12
Amina
Río Gurabo
10
18
(78)
Río Mao
Zamba
Río Amina
44
Los Quemados
Guatapanal
Las Caobas
18
21
SABANETA
Cana
Entrada de Mao
Potrero
La Cacique
Hato Viejo
13
Mata del Jobo
El Guanal
23
Clavijo
16
15
Río Yaguajal
Celestina
Jaiqui Picado
Arroyo Blanco
523
Almácigos
Gurabo
Monción
Bulla
Vidal Pichardo
SANTIAGO RODRÍGUEZ
Río Guanajuma
Río Maguá
16
El Rubio
16
San José de las Matas
(523)
Toma
815
2
Pedregal
951
Río Mao
R. Cenovi
Diferencia
SANTIAGO
Jicomé
Las Piedras
Los Monotones Abajo
1840
14
Río Amina
Mata Grande
Las Placetas
2195
Parque Nacional
Donajá
Platicos
Monte Gallo
1840
2524
Aserradero
José Armando Bermúdez
2728
2313
2801
Cda Los Gajitos
Loma La Rucilla
3045
San Pedro
2027
La Ciénaga
Monte Mijo
Pico Duarte
3175
99
103
2378
Presa de Sabaneta
Grillo
Parque Nacional

A
B
C
Santiago de Cuba
Costámbar
Punta Pastilla
Cambiaso
Punta Bajo Hondo
La Sabana
Puerto La Isla
Playa Maimón
Bahía de Maimón
Maimón
Maggiolo
Playa Cofresí
Parque Nacional Litoral Norte de Puerto Plata
Punta Cafemba
Fortaleza San Felipe
Marisol
PUERTO
Museo del Ambar
PUERTO PLATA
Las Cañas
R. Maimón
Imbert
Pico Isabel de Torres
793
Playa Dorada
Playa Sosúa
Cabo Macoris
Saballo
Boca Nueva
Puerto Plata (La Unión)
Sosúa
Parque Nacional Loma Isabel de Torres
Sabaneta de Cangrejos
Parque Nacional El Choco
Cabía
Quebrada Honda
El Cupey
Monte Llano
Loma Catalina
350
Los Arroyos
Río Camú
Tubagua
Madre Vieja
Altamira
PLATA
Los Llanos
Río Grande
Río Yásica
La Lomota
Escalera
Yásica Abajo
Jicomé Arriba
Cañada Bonita
Pontón
Pico Diego de Ocampo
1249
El Ranchito
Pedro García
Bisonó
Aguacate de Jacagua
La Toca
Palmar Abajo
La Cumbre
Los Amaceyes
Palma Herrada
Rancho de Los Plátanos
Villa Gonzáles
Jacagua
San Francisco Arriba
Palo Quemado
San Francisco Quinigua
SANTIAGO DE LOS CABALLEROS
Puerto Grande
Hatillo San Lorenzo
Santiago
San Víctor
La Canela
Museo del Tabaco
El Monumento
Tamboril
Potrero
Hato del Yaque
Pontezuela al Medio
Guamarones
El Aguacate Arriba
Jaiquí Picado
La Paloma
Licey al Medio
Cuesta Abajo
Juan López Abajo
Matanzas
MOCA
Dicayagua Abajo
Palo Amarillo
Puñal
Eugenio Perdomo
Las Carcas
Sabana de Higüerito
El Mirador
Cayetano Germosén
Los Ranchos
San José de las Matas
López
Guama
Jánico
Sabana Iglesia
Pedregal
Baitoa
Las Canas
Cutupú
Río Bao
Presa de Bao y de Tavera Yagua
La Vega Vieja
Burende
Santo Cerro
Tavera Abajo
465
Iglesia Las Mercedes
Parque Histórico La Vega Vieja
Licey
Barranca
Jamo
Bayacanes
LA VEGA
La Guama
Las Placetas
Juncalito Abajo
Sabaneta
823
Donajá
Franco Bidó
Pontón
Hatillo
Buena Vista
El Pino
Corocito
Jarabacoa
Pedregal
Río Yaque del Norte
Pinar Quemado
Salto de Jimenoa
Salto de Baiguate
La Ciénega
Manabao
Los Corozos
Sabana del Puerto
Loma Altar
1556
Reserva Científica Ebano Verde
Jima
LA VEGA
2378
Pringa
Loma Redonda
Río Masipedro
104
100

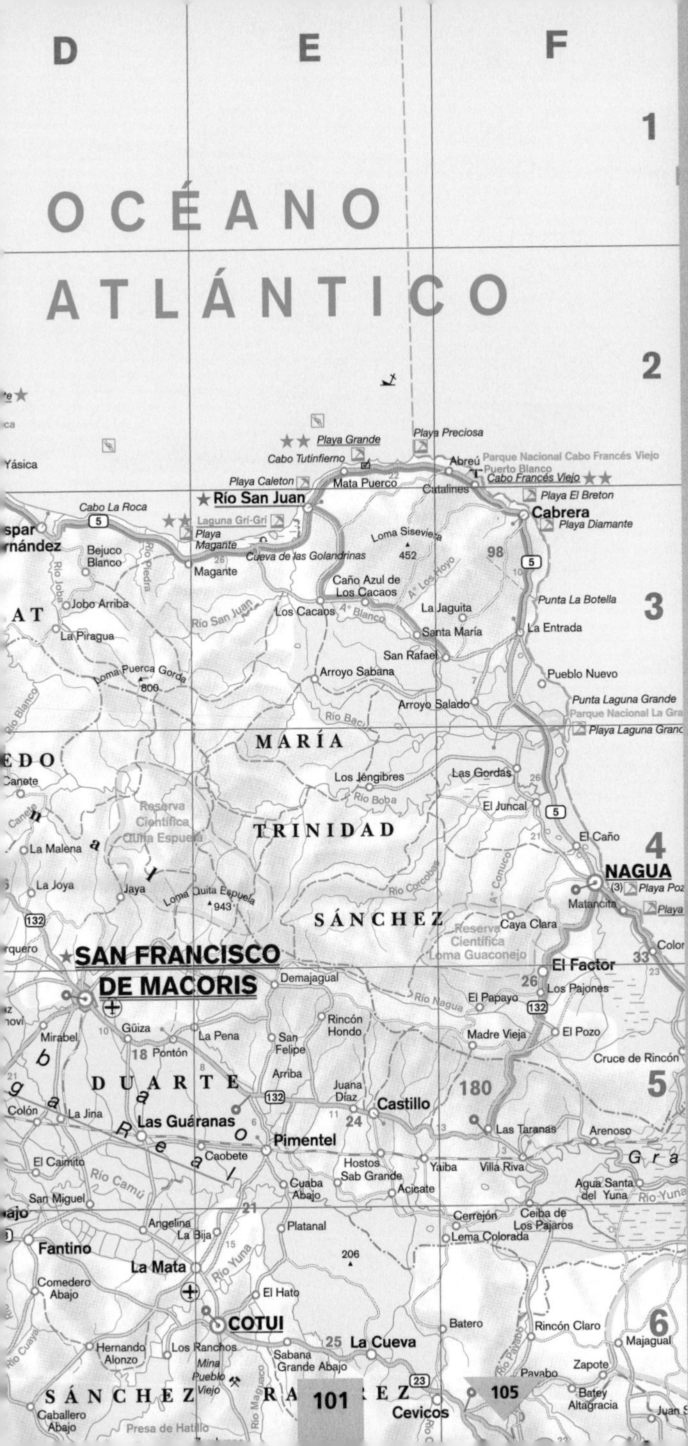
D
E
F
1
2
3
4
5
6
OCÉANO ATLÁNTICO
Playa Grande
Playa Preciosa
Cabo Tutinfierno
Abreú
Parque Nacional Cabo Francés Viejo
Puerto Blanco
Cabo Francés Viejo
Yásica
Playa Caleton
Mata Puerco
Catalines
Río San Juan
Playa El Breton
Cabo La Roca
Cabrera
Laguna Grí-Grí
Playa Diamante
Playa Magante
Loma Siseviera
452
98
Bejuco Blanco
Cueva de las Golandrinas
Magante
Caño Azul de Los Cacaos
Río Joba
Río Piedra
Punta La Botella
Jobo Arriba
Los Cacaos
La Jaguita
Río San Juan
La Entrada
Santa María
La Piragua
San Rafael
Loma Puerca Gorda
800
Arroyo Sabana
Pueblo Nuevo
Punta Laguna Grande
Arroyo Salado
Río Bací
MARÍA
Las Gordas
Los Jengibres
Río Boba
El Juncal
Canete
Reserva Científica Quita Espuela
TRINIDAD
El Caño
La Malena
NAGUA
La Joya
Jaya
Loma Quita Espuela
943
Playa Poz
Matancita
SÁNCHEZ
Caya Clara
Reserva Científica Loma Guaconejo
SAN FRANCISCO DE MACORIS
Demajagual
El Factor
Los Pajones
El Papayo
Río Nagua
Rincón Hondo
Mirabel
Güiza
La Pena
San Felipe
Madre Vieja
El Pozo
Pontón
Arriba
Cruce de Rincón
DUARTE
180
Juana Díaz
Castillo
Colón
La Jina
Las Guáranas
Las Taranas
Arenoso
Pimentel
El Caimito
Caobete
Hostos
Sab Grande
Yaiba
Villa Riva
Río Camú
Cuaba Abajo
Acicate
Agua Santa del Yuna
San Miguel
Río Yuna
Angelina
Cerrejón
Ceiba de Los Pajaros
Platanal
La Bija
Lema Colorada
Fantino
206
La Mata
Río Yuna
Comedero Abajo
El Hato
COTUI
Batero
Rincón Claro
Hernando Alonzo
Los Ranchos
La Cueva
Majagual
Mina Pueblo Viejo
Sabana Grande Abajo
Zapote
Pavabo
SÁNCHEZ RAMÍREZ
105
Batey Altagracia
Cevicos
Caballero Abajo
Presa de Hatillo
Río Maguaco

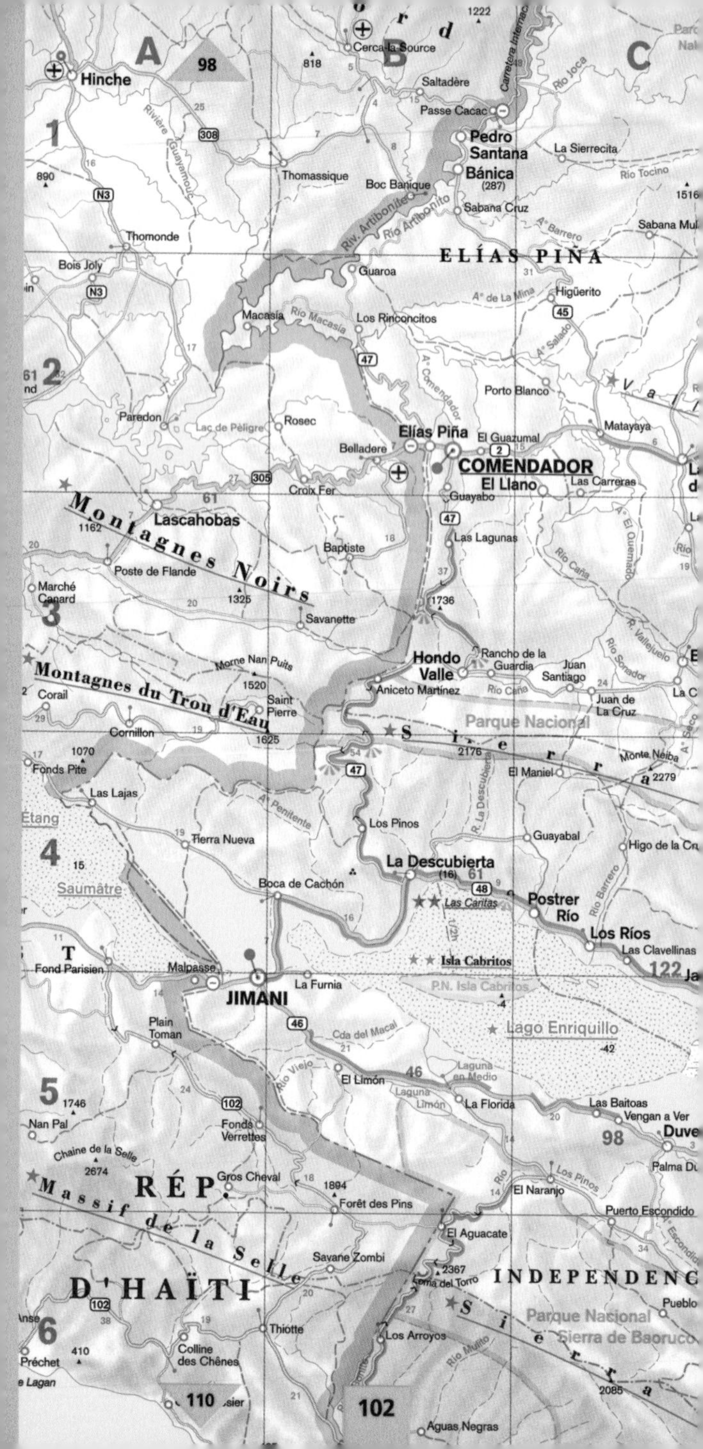

A
B
C
98
Hinche
Cerca-la-Source
Saltadère
Passe Cacac
Pedro Santana
Bánica
(287)
La Sierrecita
Río Tocino
Thomassique
Boc Banique
Sabana Cruz
Riv. Artibonite
Río Artibonito
Thomonde
Bois Joly
ELÍAS PIÑA
Guaroa
Higüerito
Macasía
Río Macasía
Los Rinconcitos
Porto Blanco
Matayaya
Paredon
Lac de Péligre
Rosec
Elías Piña
El Guazumal
Belladere
COMENDADOR
El Llano
Las Carreras
Croix Fer
Guayabo
Lascahobas
Montagnes Noirs
Las Lagunas
Baptiste
Poste de Flande
Marché Canard
Savanette
Hondo Valle
Rancho de la Guardia
Juan Santiago
Aniceto Martínez
Juan de La Cruz
Montagnes du Trou d'Eau
Morne Nan Puits
Saint Pierre
Corail
Cornillon
Parque Nacional
Sierra
Monte Neiba
El Maniel
Fonds Pite
Las Lajas
Etang Saumâtre
Los Pinos
Guayabal
Higo de la Cr
Tierra Nueva
La Descubierta
Boca de Cachón
Postrer Río
Las Caritas
Los Ríos
Las Clavellinas
Isla Cabritos
Fond Parisien
Malpasse
JIMANI
La Furnia
P.N. Isla Cabritos
Lago Enriquillo
Plain Toman
Cda del Macal
Río Viejo
El Limón
Laguna en Medio
Laguna Limón
La Florida
Las Baitoas
Vengan a Ver
Duve
Nan Pal
Fonds Verrettes
Chaine de la Selle
Palma Du
Gros Cheval
RÉP. D'HAÏTI
Forêt des Pins
El Naranjo
Los Pinos
Puerto Escondido
Massif de la Selle
El Aguacate
Savane Zombi
Loma del Torro
INDEPENDENC
Pueblo
Thiotte
Los Arroyos
Parque Nacional Sierra de Baoruco
Colline des Chênes
Préchet
Río Mulito
110
102
Aguas Negras

D
E
F
1
2
3
4
5
6
Donaja
Platicos
2524
Monte Gallo
1840
Aserradero
José Armando Bermúdez
2728
2313
2801
Cordillera Central
Cda Los Gajitos
San Pedro
2027
La Ciénaga
Monte Mijo
2276
Loma La Rucilla
3045
Pico Duarte
3175
2378
Presa de Sabaneta
Río San Juan
Sabaneta
Parque Nacional José del Carmen Ramírez
Cerro Gordo
829
El Hatico
Hato Nuevo
Guazumal
2561
Loma de la Viuda
SAN JUAN
22
Juan de Herrera
Río Yaque del Sur
El Montazo
Hato del Padre
Río Loro
Corral de los Indios
Jinova
2
33
120
Mogollón
El Ático
A° San Martín
Hato Viejo
Barranca
Chalona
SAN JUAN DE LA MAGUANA
(425)
El Coco
Bohechío
La Cumbre
Presa de Sabana Yegua
Ojo de Agua
Río Las Cuevas
Patio de
Loma de Jayaco
1472
1692
Cuenda
A° Agua Salada
R. San Juan
Sabana Alta
Guanito
Padre Las Casas
Cardón
Río Los Baos
49
Los Corozos
A° Salado
Los Bancos
Rancho Copey
Vallejuelo
Sabana Grande
Hato Viejo
Capá
27
Villarpando
Bastidas
19
Río Vieiama
1842
Cabeza de Toro
El Oregano Grande
Magueyal
Yayas de Viajama
Arroyo Blanco
Hato Nuevo
N e i b a
BAORUCO
A° Guanarate
Los Toros
Las Guanabanas
Galván
Guanarate
El Mamón
Río Mejía
El Rodeo
31
Orégano Chiquito
El Salado
Río Yaque del Sur
42
32
Tábara Abajo
NEIBA
48
44
Quita Conaza
Fondo Negro
R. Las Lajas
Río Blanco
San Antonio
El Palmar
19
62
Tamayo
Vincente Noble
Parque Nacional Sierra Martín García
Lago de Neiba
Canal Charco Largo
Uvilla
Monte Busú
1343
A° Chupadero
Fondo Negro
Mena
El Jobo
Canoa
Sierra Martín García
Loma del Aguacate
1284
Palma Buena
21
46
11
Parque Nacional Lagunа del Rincón
Laguna del Rincón
Jaquimeyes
El Peñón
Palo Alto
Lago La Sierra
Alejandro
A° Mordán
Barreras
Angostura
Cristobal
Las Salinas
52
Fundación
La Hoya
Bahía de Neiba
Lemba
Cachón
Los Saladillos
Tierra Blanca
Cabral
Punta Martín García
BARAHONA
(10)
La Guázara
1670
Parque Nacional
Playa de Barahona
Payaso

99
111

A
B
C
100
1
2
3
4
5
6
Donajá
Franco Bidó
Hatillo
Pontón
El Pino
Buena Vista
Jarabacoa
Pedregal
Corocito
Río Yaque del Norte
Pinar Quemado
Salto de Jimenoa
Salto de Baiguate
Sabana del Puerto
La Ciénega
Manabao
Los Corozos
Loma Altar
1556
Reserva Científica Ebano Verde
Jima
Pringar
LA VEGA
2378
Loma Redonda
2295
2143
Río Yaquecillo
A° Grande
El Río
Río Jimenoa
Río Masipedro
La Cotorra
BONAO
(173)
Tireo Abajo
Constanza
(1212)
Palero
Loma Arroyo Toro
1565
La Salvia
MONSEÑOR
Río Tireo
La Union
Río Blanco
Blanco
Salto de Agua Blanca
Monte Culo de Maco
2229
Río Grande
Presa Alto Yuna
Valle Nuevo
Alto Bandera
2848
Río Nizao
Parque Nacional Valle Nuevo
La Siembra
Río Guayabal
Loma de la Chorreosa
2453
La Cumbre
El Guayabal
Patio de Dios
1358
Padre Las Casas
Monte Bonito
Las Guamas
Loma de la Lechuga
2672
Palma Cana
La Nuez
Rancho A
Las Avispas
Río Las Cuevas
Loma Piquito
1710
Monte Tetero Mejía
2581
Sierra de Ocoa
Loma El Muñeco
1711
Las Lagunitas
Valle de Río Ocoa
La Horma
1222
Viajama
A° Viajama
Río Jura
A° Hondo
AZUA
Yayas de Viajama
Nizao
Peralta
El Cecado
Río El Canal
Río Ocoa
Tabara Arriba
La Ciénaga
Los Toros
Sajanoa
El Carrizal
Rancho del Pino
El Pinar
San José de Ocoa
Las Guanabanas
Puerto
Las Lomas
Río Banilejo
Río Grande
Las Yayitas
El Memiso
Los Anones
Orégano Chiquito
La Altagracia
A° Copey
PERA
AZUA de Compostela
(83)
Río Vía
Cañada Cimarrona
Los Ranchitos
1715
El Cruce del Quince
Sabana Yegua
Estebania
Las Charcas
Los Jovillos
Clavellina
R. Las Lajas
Río Tábara
Antonio
Monte Río
Puerto Tortuguero
Playa Monte Río
A° Hatillo
Presa de Sabana Buey
Los Ranchitos
Pueblo Viejo
Playa Blanca
Hatillo
El Número
360
A° Chupadero
El Rosario
Bahía de Ocoa
Palmar de Buena Vista
Puerto Viejo de Azua
Punta Vigía
Carbonito
El Número
628
Las Carreras
139
Cayo Boca Chica
Cayo Puerto Viejo
Cayo Agua Dulce
Galeón
Barreras
Palmar de Ocoa
Punta Ocoa
Villa Fundación
Sabana Buey
García
Bahía de Las Calderas
Arroyo Hondo
Punta Salina
Las Salinas
Las Calderas
Playa Las Salinas
Punta Santanilla
Parque Nacional Dunas de Las Calderas

Pimentel
El Caimito
Caobete
Hostos
Sab Grande
Yaiba
101
Agua Santa del Yuna
Río Yuna
San Miguel
Río Camú
Cuaba Abajo
Acicate
Angelina
La Bija
Platanal
Cerrejón
Ceiba de Los Pajaros
Lema Colorada
Fantino
La Mata
Río Yuna
206
Comedero Abajo
El Hato
COTUI
Batero
Rincón Claro
Majagual
Hernando Alonzo
Los Ranchos
Mina Pueblo Viejo
Sabana Grande Abajo
La Cueva
Río Payabo
Payabo
Zapote
Batey Altagracia
SÁNCHEZ RAMÍREZ
Cevicos
Caballero Abajo
Presa de Hatillo
Río Maguaca
Río Cevicos
Juan S
La Trinchera 592
Zambrana Abajo
Abadesa
Sabana
Hatillo
Chacuey Maldonado
Río Chacuey
Cabeza de Toro
Las Lagunas
Loma Culo del Diablo 496
Sabana de Payabo
Loma la Guardarraya 592
Loma Media Cara 526
La Guàzuma
Frías
El Dean
Piedra Blanca
Río Ozama
Don Juan
Guazumita
MONTE
La Jagua
Cacique
La Jina
Esperalvillo
Hato Arriba
Pino Herrado
Río Yamasá
El Rincón
La Guia
Río Verde
San Antonio
Yamasá (82)
Los Jovillos
Las Matas
Río Guanuma
Los Botados
Guanuma
Río Haina
Básima
Río Higuero
Hato Viejo
San Mateo
Río La Savila
Villa Altagracía
250
La Jina
Madrigal
Río Yuca
Higuero
La Bomba
Río Maná
Río Isa
El Cidral
San Felipe
El Caobal
Río Isabela
Hatillo
El Cajuilito
La Victoria
Presa de Madrigal
Calderón
DISTRITO NACIO
SAN CRISTÓBAL
Medina
Río Haina
La Isabela
Villa Mella
Río Ozama
San Francisco
Los Alcarrizos
Jardín Botánico
Parque Zoológico
Cancino
El Guineo
Hato Damas
Mendoza
La Cabirma
Manoguayabo
Faro a Colón
Mano Matuey
La Colonia
El Tablazo
Palabe
Plaza de la Cultura
Zona Colonial
Los Tres Ojos
Cambita Pueblecito
P.N. Cuevas de Borbón
La Pared
Santo Domingo (Herrera)
Acuario Nacional
Cambita Garabitos
La Toma
SANTO DOMINGO
Casa de Caoba
P.N. Litoral Sur de Santo Domingo
Humachón
Presa de Valdesia
Hatillo
Bajos de Haína
Najayo Arriba
SAN CRISTÓBAL (33)
Valdesia
Nigua
Las Gallardas
San Gregorio de Nigua
Boca de Nigua
Cueva Santa María
Las Barías
El Conde
Yaguate
Cribití
Limonal
Playa Najayo
Pizarrete
Najayo Abajo
Carretón
R. Nizao
Bahía de Najayo
Lucas Díaz
Najayo
Raya
Santana
Sabana Grande de Palenque
Nizao
Juan Barón
Playa Palenque
Punta Palenque
Punta Catalina
Playa Nizao
Diómedes Imperial
Colón (Panamá)
La Guaira (Venezuela)

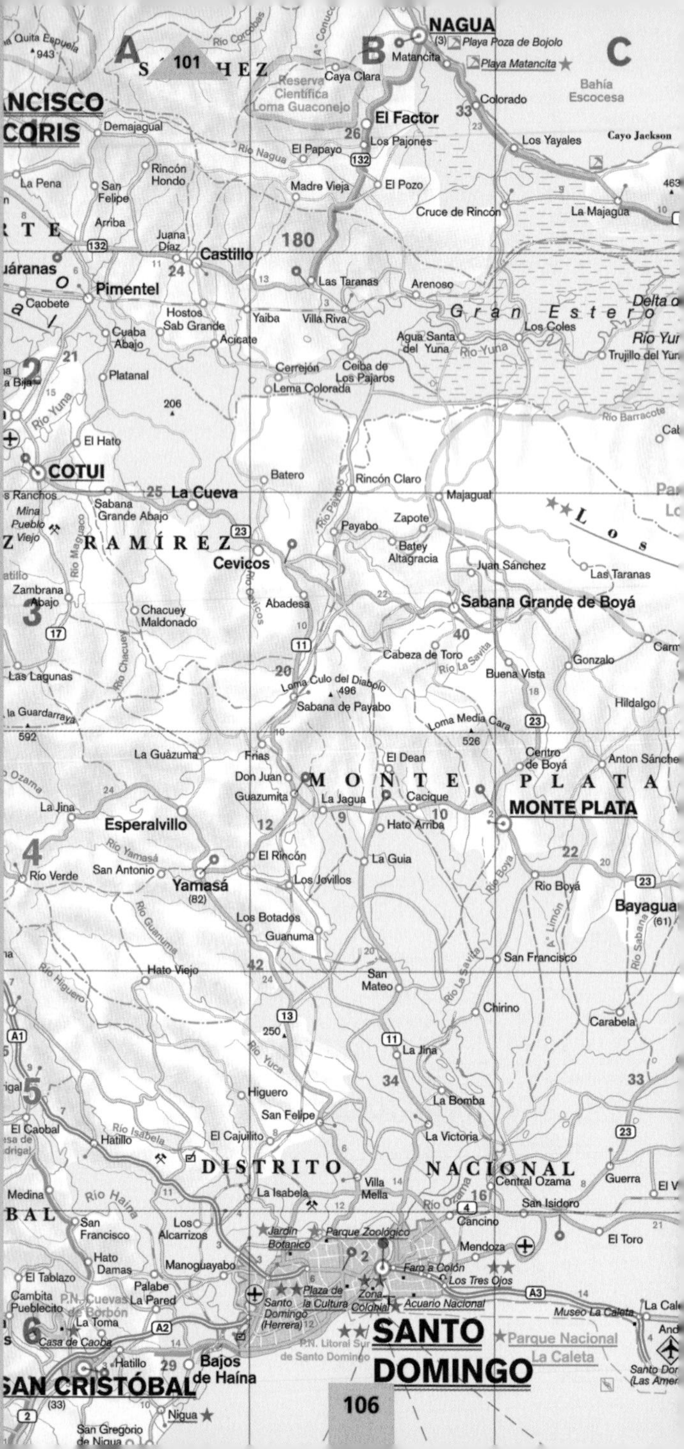A
B
C
101
SÁNCHEZ
NAGUA
Playa Poza de Bojolo
Matancita
Playa Matancita
Reserva Científica Loma Guaconejo
Caya Clara
Bahía Escocesa
Colorado
El Factor
Los Pajones
Los Yayales
Cayo Jackson
Demajagual
Río Nagua
El Papayo
Rincón Hondo
La Pena
San Felipe
Madre Vieja
El Pozo
Cruce de Rincón
La Majagua
Arriba
Juana Díaz
180
Castillo
Pimentel
Caobete
Las Taranas
Arenoso
Hostos
Sab Grande
Yaiba
Villa Riva
Gran Estero
Delta
Cuaba Abajo
Acicate
Agua Santa del Yuna
Río Yuna
Los Coles
Trujillo del Yuna
Cerrejón
Ceiba de Los Pajaros
Lema Colorada
Platanal
206
Río Barracote
El Hato
COTUI
Batero
Rincón Claro
Ranchos
La Cueva
Majagual
Sabana Grande Abajo
Mina Pueblo Viejo
Río Payabo
Payabo
Zapote
Los
RAMÍREZ
Cevicos
Batey Altagracia
Juan Sánchez
Las Taranas
Zambrana Abajo
Chacuey Maldonado
Río Maguaco
Río Cevicos
Abadesa
Sabana Grande de Boyá
3
Río Chacuey
Cabeza de Toro
Río La Savita
Buena Vista
Gonzalo
Las Lagunas
Loma Culo del Diablo
496
Sabana de Payabo
Hildalgo
la Guardarraya
592
Loma Media Cara
526
La Guàzuma
Frias
El Dean
Centro de Boyá
Anton Sánchez
Ozama
Don Juan
Guazumita
MONTE PLATA
La Jagua
Cacique
MONTE PLATA
La Jina
Esperalvillo
Hato Arriba
4
Río Yamasá
El Rincón
La Guia
Río Verde
San Antonio
Yamasá
(82)
Los Jovillos
Río Boyá
Río Boyá
Bayaguana
(61)
Río Guanuma
Los Botados
Guanuma
A° Limón
Río Sabana
San Francisco
Hato Viejo
Río Higuero
San Mateo
Río La Savita
Chirino
Carabela
250
Río Yuca
La Jina
A1
5
Higuero
La Bomba
San Felipe
El Caobal
Hatillo
Río Isabela
El Cajuilito
La Victoria
DISTRITO NACIONAL
Central Ozama
Guerra
Medina
Río Haina
La Isabela
Villa Mella
Río Ozama
BAL
San Francisco
Los Alcarrizos
San Isidoro
Cancino
Jardín Botanico
Parque Zoológico
Mendoza
El Toro
Hato Damas
Manoguayabo
El Tablazo
Faro a Colón
Los Tres Ojos
Palabe
Cambita Pueblecito
P.N. Cuevas de Borbón
La Pared
Plaza de la Cultura
Zona Colonial
Acuario Nacional
A3
Santo Domingo (Herrera)
Museo La Caleta
La Caleta
La Toma
A2
6
Casa de Caoba
P.N. Litoral Sur de Santo Domingo
SANTO DOMINGO
Parque Nacional La Caleta
Santo Domingo (Las Américas)
Hatillo
Bajos de Haina
SAN CRISTÓBAL
(33)
106
Nigua
San Gregorio de Nigua

D
E
F
1
2
3
4
5
6
Cabo Cabrón
Playa Rincón
Punta Mala
Monte La Meseta
606
Bahía del Rincón
Playa Cozón
Playa El Portillo
Punta El Estillero
Cayo Limón
Cayo Canas
Punta Ermitaño
Puerto del Valle
Playa Las Galeras
Punta El Cabito
Cabo Samaná
El Portillo
Barbacos
El Limón
El Valle
Monte Pan de Azúcar
493
Las Galeras
Punta Vaca
SAMANÁ
546
Saltos de Limón
Península de Samaná
Monte Diablo
349
Playa Playuela
Juana Vicenta
Salto Río Los Cocos
SANTA BÁRBARA DE SAMANÁ
Puerto Francès Viejo
Las Garitas
Los Róbalos
Las Pascualas
Honduras
Los Cacaos
El Francès
Arroyo Barril
Punta Mangle
Punta Balandra
Punta de Los Corozos
Cayo La Farola
Cayo Arenas
Cayo Levantado
Bahía de Samaná
Punta El Negro
Bahía de San Lorenzo
Punta Yabón
Conde de Tolosa
Cuevas de Caño Hondo (Cueva de la Línea)
Sabana de la Mar
Nuestra Señora de Guadalupe
Punta Capitán
Punta El Morro
Punta Mangles
Capitán
Punta Ratón
Bahía de La Jina
El Caño
Las Cañitas
Punta Jayán
Playa Miches
El Centro
Maguá
HATO
Río Yanigua
El Valle
La Loma
El Morro
Miches
Arenitas
Río Catalina
Río Maguá
Río Jayán
Cordillera Oriental
La Deseada
469
603
San Rafael
La Loma
Pedro Sánchez
Río Guaquía
Vicentillo
Río Seibo
Sierra
Trinidad
Sabana de Barriolo
Río Magarín
Río Almirante
MAYOR
Manchado
Río Ciabo
EL SEÍBO
Magarín
Candelaria
Yabacao
Río Yabacao
Yerbabuena
HATO MAYOR
El Puerto
221
Dos Rios
San Geronimo
Cibahuete
La Higüera
Río Azui
Las Pajas
Río Anamá
El Higo
Juana Lorenzo
Guayabo Dulce
Los Algarrobos
Río Tosa
Los Jibaros
Río Iguamo
Covadonga
Batey Guayacanes
Sabanas del Soco
Los Llanos
Campiña
Ulloa
129
Llano de Seibo
Platanitos
Río Caganche
Río Soco
Batey Lechuga
Los Montones
Río Iguamo
Río Maguá
Consuelo
Regajo
Diego
Los Lerenes
Ramón Santana
Quisqueya
A° Lima
La Yeguada
Ing. Anquelina
La Balsa
Magarín
La Mula
Los Montes
SAN PEDRO DE MACORÍS
Higüera
P.N. Cuevas Las Maravillas
Ing. Cristobál Colón
Tintero
Honduras
Ingenio Porvenir
Boca del Soco
Jagual
Río Cumayasa
Soco
Chica
La Punta
San Pedro Apostol
Caribe
Guayacanes
Juan Dolio
Playa Boca del Soco
Los Arados
SAN PEDRO DE MACORÍS
Playa de Juan Dolio
Playa Villas del Mar
Punta Mortero
LA ROMANA
Playa Guayacanes
Cumayasa
Punta Magdalena
Playa Cumayasa
Punta Blanca
Playas del Este
Punta Pérez

108

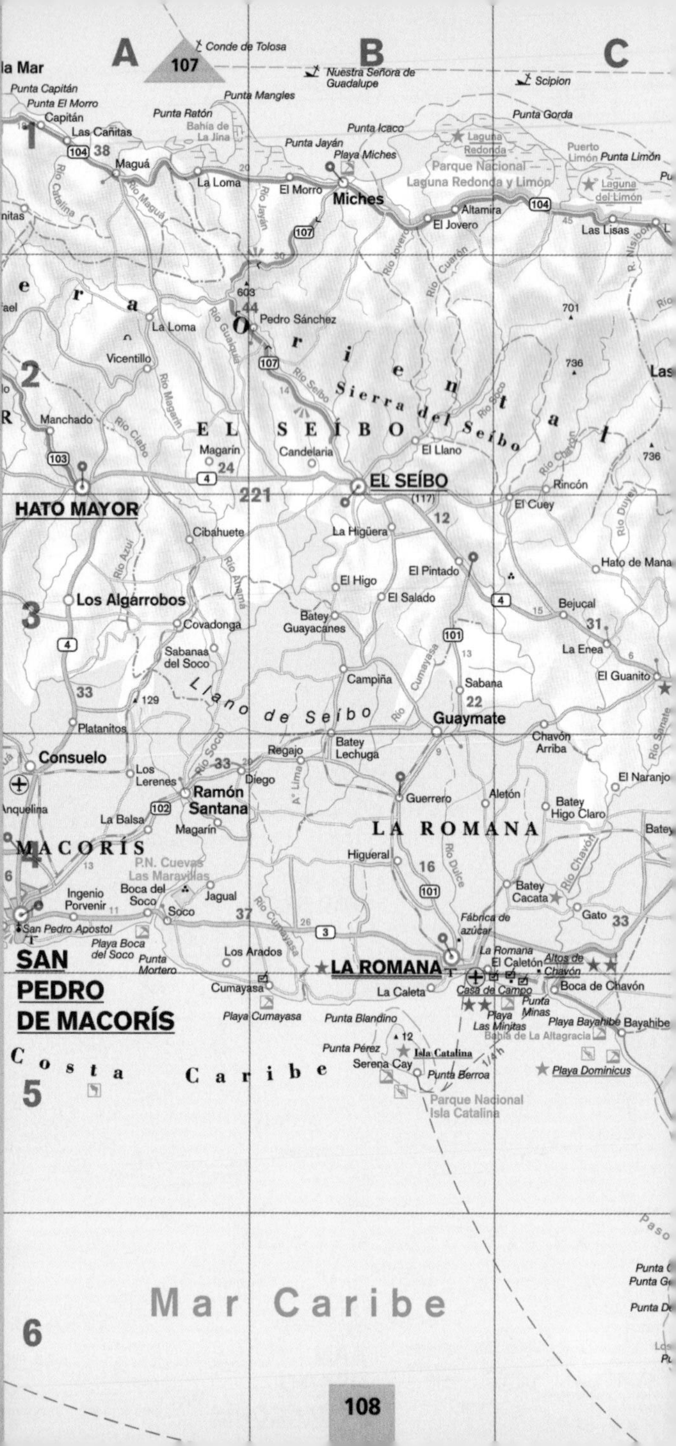
A
B
C
107
Conde de Tolosa
Nuestra Señora de Guadalupe
Scipion
la Mar
Punta Capitán
Punta El Morro
Capitán
Las Cañitas
104
38
Punta Mangles
Punta Ratón
Bahía de La Jina
Punta Icaco
Punta Jayán
Playa Miches
Punta Gorda
Laguna Redonda
Parque Nacional Laguna Redonda y Limón
Puerto Limón
Punta Limón
Laguna del Limón
Maguá
La Loma
El Morro
Miches
Altamira
El Jovero
Las Lisas
Río Catalina
Río Maguá
Río Jayán
Río Jovero
Río Cuarón
R. Nisibón
603
44
Pedro Sánchez
La Loma
Vicentillo
Río Guaiquía
Río Magarín
701
736
Cordillera Oriental
Sierra del Seíbo
Río Seibo
Río Soco
Manchado
Río Ciabo
EL SEÍBO
Magarín
Candelaria
El Llano
24
221
Río Chavón
Rincón
103
4
HATO MAYOR
EL SEÍBO
117
El Cuey
12
Río Duyey
Cibahuete
La Higüera
Hato de Mana
Río Azuí
Río Anamá
El Pintado
El Higo
Los Algarrobos
El Salado
Bejucal
31
Covadonga
Batey Guayacanes
101
La Enea
Sabanas del Soco
El Guanito
Cumayasa
13
Campiña
Sabana
22
33
129
Llano de Seíbo
Platanitos
Guaymate
Chavón Arriba
Río Sanate
Consuelo
Regajo
Batey Lechuga
Los Lerenes
33
Diego
Ramón Santana
Río Soco
A° Lima
Guerrero
Aletón
El Naranjo
Batey Higo Claro
Anquelina
102
La Balsa
Magarín
LA ROMANA
Batey
MACORÍS
P.N. Cuevas Las Maravillas
Higueral
16
Río Dulce
Ingenio Porvenir
Boca del Soco
Jagual
Batey Cacata
101
Río Chavón
Soco
37
Río Cumayasa
Fábrica de azúcar
Gato
33
San Pedro Apostol
3
Playa Boca del Soco
Punta Mortero
Los Arados
La Romana
El Caletón
Altos de Chavón
SAN PEDRO DE MACORÍS
LA ROMANA
Cumayasa
La Caleta
Casa de Campo
Boca de Chavón
Playa Cumayasa
Punta Blandino
Playa Las Minitas
Punta Minas
Playa Bayahibe
Bayahibe
Bahía de La Altagracia
12
Punta Pérez
Isla Catalina
Serena Cay
Punta Berroa
Playa Dominicus
Costa Caribe
Parque Nacional Isla Catalina
1/4 h
1
2
3
4
5
6
Paso
Mar Caribe

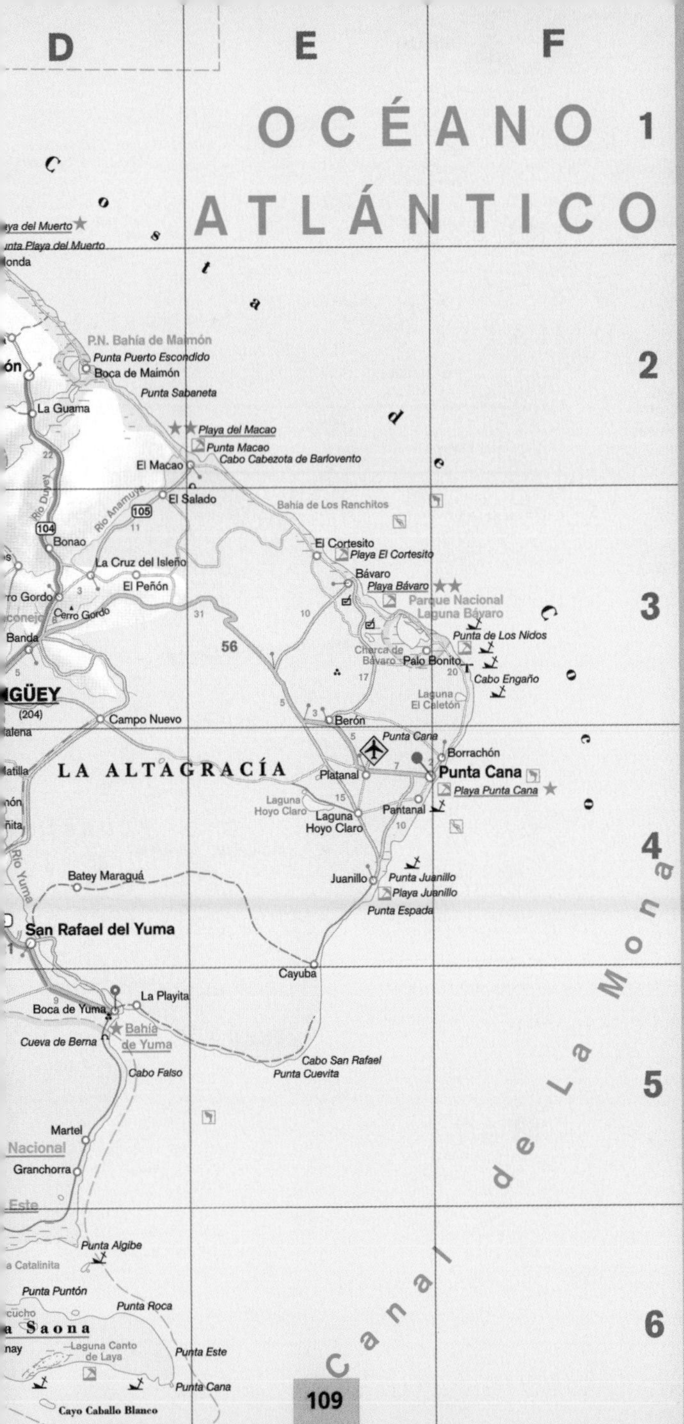
D
E
F
OCÉANO ATLÁNTICO
1
2
3
4
5
6
Costa de Coco
Canal de La Mona
Playa del Muerto
Punta Playa del Muerto
P.N. Bahía de Maimón
Punta Puerto Escondido
Boca de Maimón
Punta Sabaneta
La Guama
Playa del Macao
Punta Macao
Cabo Cabezota de Barlovento
El Macao
El Salado
Río Duyey
Río Anamuya
105
104
Bonao
Bahía de Los Ranchitos
El Cortesito
Playa El Cortesito
La Cruz del Isleño
El Peñón
Bávaro
Playa Bávaro
Parque Nacional Laguna Bávaro
Cerro Gordo
Banda
56
Punta de Los Nidos
Charca de Bávaro
Palo Bonito
Cabo Engaño
Laguna El Caletón
(204)
Campo Nuevo
Berón
Punta Cana
Borrachón
LA ALTAGRACÍA
Platanal
Punta Cana
Playa Punta Cana
Laguna Hoyo Claro
Laguna Hoyo Claro
Pantanal
Río Yuma
Batey Maraguá
Juanillo
Punta Juanillo
Playa Juanillo
Punta Espada
San Rafael del Yuma
Cayuba
La Playita
Boca de Yuma
Bahía de Yuma
Cueva de Berna
Cabo Falso
Cabo San Rafael
Punta Cuevita
Martel
Nacional
Granchorra
Este
Punta Algibe
Catalinita
Punta Puntón
Punta Roca
Saona
Laguna Canto de Laya
Punta Este
Punta Cana
Cayo Caballo Blanco

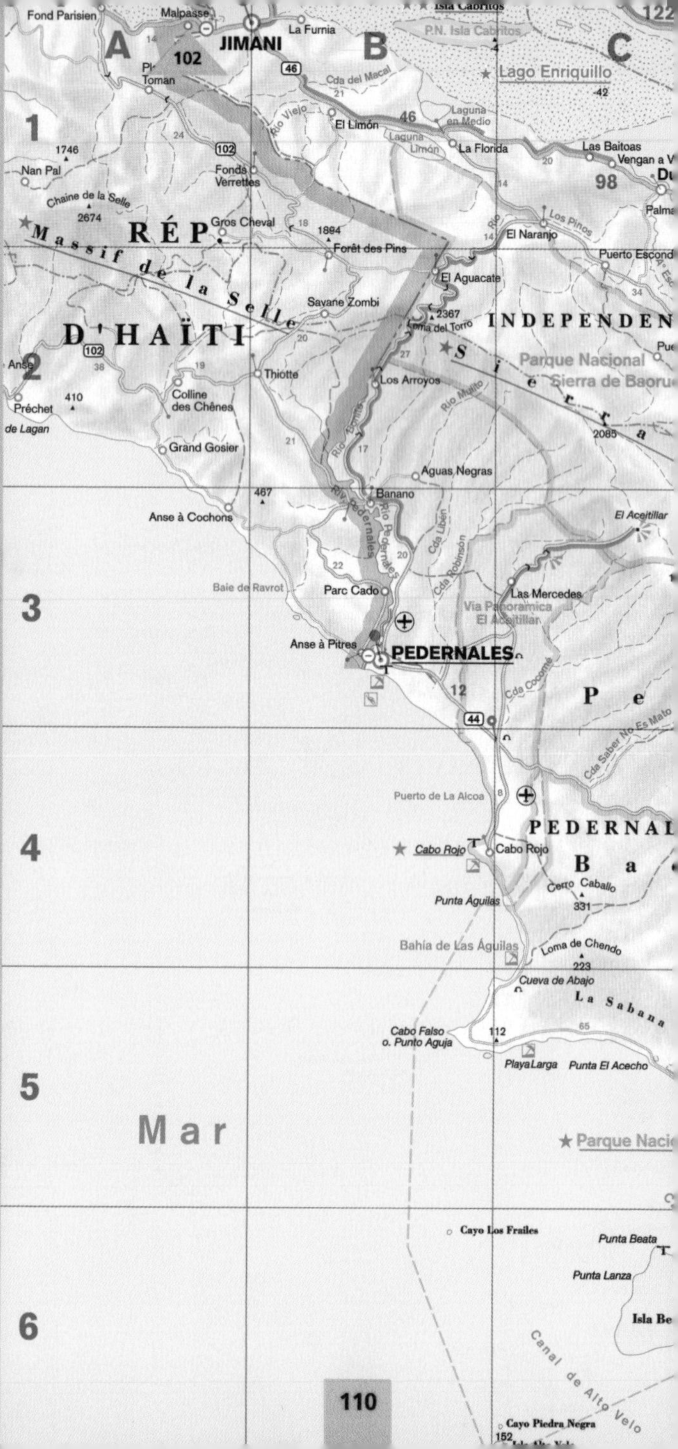
Fond Parisien
Malpasse
La Furnia
P.N. Isla Cabritos
Isla Cabritos
A
B
C
102
JIMANI
46
Toman
Cda del Macal
Lago Enriquillo
-42
-4
1
Rio Viejo
El Limón
46
Laguna en Medio
Laguna Limón
La Florida
Las Baitoas
1746
Nan Pal
Fonds Verrettes
98
Chaine de la Selle
2674
Gros Cheval
RÉP.
1894
Forêt des Pins
El Naranjo
Los Pinos
Puerto Escond
Massif de la Selle
El Aguacate
Savane Zombi
2367
Loma del Torro
INDEPENDEN
D'HAÏTI
Parque Nacional Sierra de Baoru
2
Thiotte
Los Arroyos
Rio Mulito
Sierra
Préchet
410
Colline des Chênes
de Lagan
2085
Grand Gosier
Rio Bonito
Aguas Negras
467
Banano
Anse à Cochons
Rio Pedernales
El Aceitillar
Cda Libén
Cda Robinson
Baie de Ravrot
Parc Cado
Las Mercedes
3
Via Panoramica El Aceitillar
Anse à Pitres
PEDERNALES
12
Cda Cocomé
Pe
44
Cda Saber No Es Mato
Puerto de La Alcoa
PEDERNAL
4
Cabo Rojo
Cabo Rojo
Ba
Cerro Caballo
331
Punta Águilas
Bahía de Las Águilas
Loma de Chendo
223
Cueva de Abajo
La Sabana
65
Cabo Falso
o. Punto Aguja
112
Playa Larga
Punta El Acecho
5
Mar
Parque Naci
Cayo Los Frailes
Punta Beata
Punta Lanza
6
Isla Be
Canal de Alto Velo
Cayo Piedra Negra
152

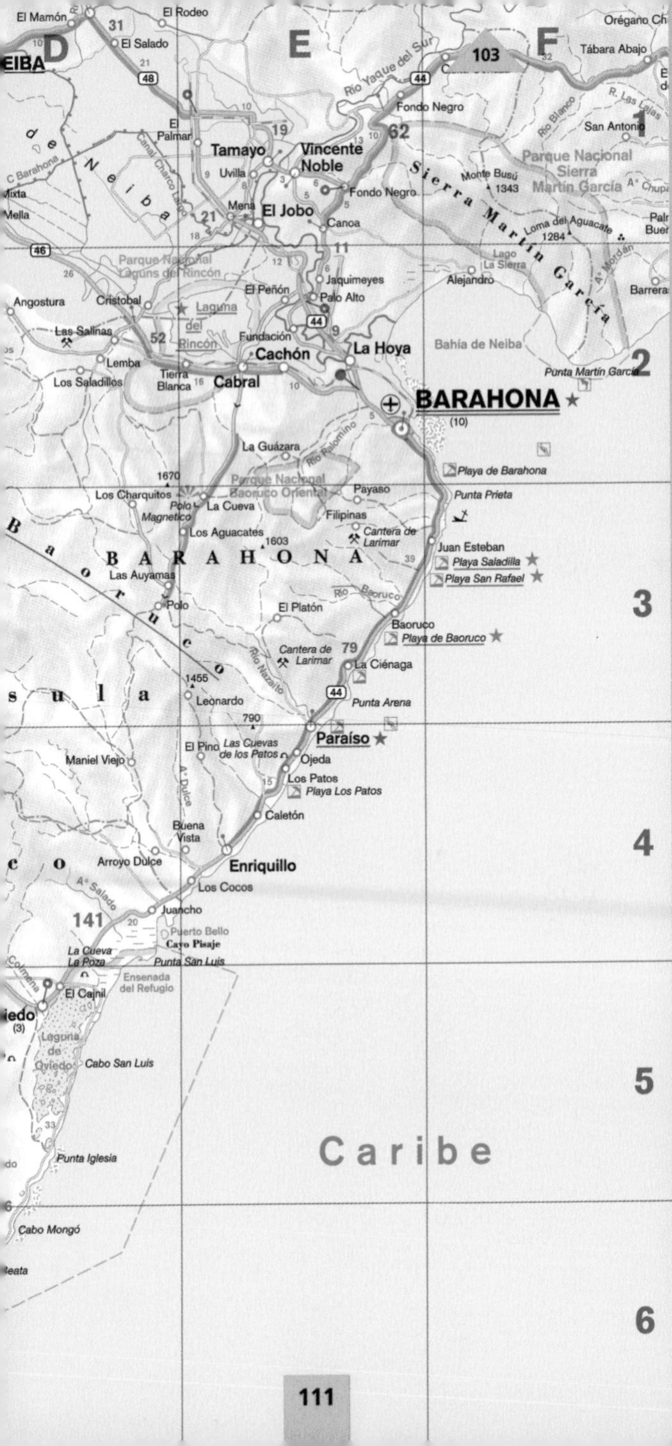
D
E
F
103
EIBA
El Mamón
El Rodeo
El Salado
Orégano Chico
Tábara Abajo
Río Yaque del Sur
Fondo Negro
Río Blanco
R. Las Lajas
San Antonio
El Palmar
Tamayo
Vincente Noble
Uvilla
Fondo Negro
Canal Charco Largo
Sierra Martín García
Monte Busú 1343
Parque Nacional Sierra Martín García
Mixta
Mella
Mena
El Jobo
Canoa
Loma del Aguacate 1284
C Barahona
Parque Nacional Laguna del Rincón
Lago La Sierra
Alejandro
A° Mordán
Barrera
Angostura
Cristobal
El Peñón
Jaquimeyes
Palo Alto
Laguna del Rincón
Las Salinas
Fundación
Cachón
La Hoya
Bahía de Neiba
Lemba
Los Saladillos
Tierra Blanca
Cabral
Punta Martín García
BARAHONA
(10)
Río Palomino
La Guázara
Playa de Barahona
Parque Nacional Baoruco Oriental
Payaso
Punta Prieta
1670
Los Charquitos
Polo Magnetico
La Cueva
Filipinas
Cantera de Larimar
Los Aguacates
1603
Juan Esteban
B A R A H O N A
Playa Saladilla
Playa San Rafael
Las Auyamas
Río Baoruco
Polo
El Platón
Baoruco
Playa de Baoruco
Cantera de Larimar
La Ciénaga
Río Nazaito
1455
Leonardo
Punta Arena
790
El Pino
Las Cuevas de los Patos
Paraíso
Maniel Viejo
Ojeda
Los Patos
Playa Los Patos
A° Dulce
Caletón
Buena Vista
Arroyo Dulce
Enriquillo
Los Cocos
A° Salado
Juancho
Puerto Bello
Cayo Pisaje
La Cueva
La Poza
Punta San Luis
Ensenada del Refugio
El Cajnil
Laguna de Oviedo
Cabo San Luis
Caribe
Punta Iglesia
Cabo Mongó
1
2
3
4
5
6